BUDDHISM

Clive Erricker

TEACH YOURSELF BOOKS

For UK orders: please contact Bookpoint Ltd, 39 Milton Park, Abingdon, Oxon OX14 4TD. Telephone: (44) 01235 400414, Fax: (44) 01235 400454. Lines are open from 9.00 – 6.00, Monday to Saturday, with a 24 hour message answering service. Email address: orders@bookpoint.co.uk

For U.S.A. & Canada orders: please contact NTC/Contemporary Publishing, 4255 West Touhy Avenue, Lincolnwood, Illinois 60646 – 1975 U.S.A. Telephone: (847) 679 5500, Fax: (847) 679 2494.

Long-renowned as the authoritative source for self-guided learning – with more than 30 million copies sold worldwide – the *Teach Yourself* series includes over 200 titles in the fields of languages, crafts, hobbies, sports, and other leisure activities.

British Library Cataloguing in Publication Data
A catalogue record for this title is available from The British Library

Library of Congress Catalog Card Number: 95–82513

First published in UK 1995 by Hodder Headline Plc, 338 Euston Road, London NW1 3BH

First published in US 1995 by NTC/Contemporary Publishing, 4255 West Touhy Avenue, Lincolnwood (Chicago), Illinois 60646 – 1975 U.S.A.

The 'Teach Yourself' name and logo are registered trade marks of Hodder & Stoughton Ltd.

Typeset by Transet Limited, Coventry, Warwickshire.
Printed in Great Britain for Hodder & Stoughton Educational, a division of Hodder Headline Plc, 338 Euston Road, London NW1 3BH by Cox & Wyman Ltd, Reading, Berkshire.

Impression number	16	15	14	13	12	11	10	9
Year		2004	2003	2002	2001	2000	1999	

CONTENTS

Acknowledgements

To Jane for encouragement and criticism, hard work
on the word-processor and forgiveness.
To Katy, Sam and Polly for putting up with it all.
To Karin for generously making the offer.
To Karunavira for the interviews.

The publishers would like to thank the following for their permission to reproduce copyright photographs and artwork in this book:
P J A Veale, FWBO – p. 171; C Erricker – pp. 26, 31, 46, 61, 98, 138, 149, 159, 172; Tantra Designs and Computers Ltd – p. 66; P Gold, Wisdom Publications – pp. 96, 140; Dharmachari Aloka – p. 46.

— INTRODUCTION —

This book is about what Buddhists think, what they do, and how they live their lives. This varies according to the type of Buddhism that is practised and where each Buddhist lives; essentially, however, all Buddhists follow the teachings of the Buddha – the Fully Enlightened One – as they have been transmitted over the last 2,500 years. Varied sources have been drawn on in order to evoke the spirit of Buddhism and allow Buddhists to speak for themselves.

Buddhism today is very diverse; this diversity contributes to its richness, and nowhere more so than in the West. Moreover, Buddhism offers teachings and practices that are open to anyone with a little intellectual curiosity and the willingness to accept that the modern world can benefit from ancient and timeless wisdom.

Note on terminology

Due to the difference in languages used by the Theravadin and Mahayanist branches of Buddhism, (Pali and Sanskrit respectively), Buddhist terms can appear in two forms: for example, *Dhamma* (Pali) and *Dharma* (Sanskrit). The Buddha's name also varies accordingly: Siddhatta Gotama (Pali) and Siddhartha Gautama (Sanskrit). The glossary indicates the alternative renditions of terms used in this book.

1
BUDDHISTS AND BUDDHISM

Thus shall ye think of all this fleeting world:
A star at dawn, a bubble in a stream,
A flash of lightning in a summer cloud,
A flickering lamp, a phantom, and a dream.

Who are Buddhists?

This is a question that many people in the West might well ask. The quotation above is from the Buddha himself, and one answer to our question is that Buddhists are those who understand the world in this way. But such a statement is easily misunderstood, so perhaps we should start by approaching our question in a less poetic fashion.

How would Buddhists today answer it? Some might reply that Buddhists are the followers of the Buddha and his teachings. Whilst this is an accurate response, it is open to misunderstanding. For example, Buddhists do not follow the Buddha in the same way as Christians follow Christ. The reason for this is that the Buddha is not understood to be a God; nor did he teach his disciples a way to God. Indeed, he did not even claim that his teachings were a unique and original source of wisdom; but he did maintain that they had a very specific practical purpose and that they were meant to be useful.

Buddha always said, 'Don't take what I'm saying, just try to analyse as far as possible and see whether what I'm saying makes sense or not. If it doesn't make sense, discard it. If it does make sense, then pick it up.'

(John Bowker, *Worlds of Faith*, BBC, 1983, p 134)

Another way of answering the question might be to say that Buddhists practise the *Dhamma* (Pali) or *Dharma* (Sanskrit). This word has a range of meanings that interconnect. Most importantly, dharma means truth, law or teaching. Thus, Buddhists are stressing that the Buddha's teaching pointed to the truth; and moreover, that they are practising what the Buddha preached, truthful living, which is open to everyone.

The *Dhamma* can be practised by anybody. It can be practised by any man, woman, even by any child. It can be practised by someone in India, and it can be practised by someone in England. By someone in America, or someone in China. If there are people on the moon, it can be practised by those people on the moon. The *Dhamma* is universal . . . it's for everybody – for every human being. Because every human being is the brother or sister of every other human being. The more we practise the *Dhamma*, the more we come together. It doesn't matter whether we are born in India or whether we are born in England. If we practise the *Dhamma*, we are one. If we practise the *Dhamma*, we are brothers and sisters.

(Ven. Sangharakshita, *Friends of the Western Buddhist Order*, Newsletter no.54, p 2)

A third answer to the question would be to say that Buddhists are those who belong to the *Sangha*. Sangha means community. Often it denotes the monastic community, but in a broader sense it refers to Buddhists in general. It could be said that Buddhists are part of the Sangha in the way that Christians belong to the Church. However, the distinction of belonging to the Buddhist community is a commitment to living a life that cultivates well-being and happiness through following particular teachings, rules and practices. Sometimes the members of the Sangha are referred to as 'spiritual friends'.

For twenty-five centuries the Community has held Buddhism together. It is a refuge for the weary and an ideal of renunciation, a source of leadership and a standard of permanence in times of cultural change. It is an institution, and thus always available to those who need it. The religious vocation is given a home, the seeker is given a path, and the life of brotherhood is established as a model for all mankind.

(Stephan Beyer, *The Buddhist Experience*, Dickenson, 1974, p 65)

If we put all three answers together we arrive at a more complete understanding of what it means to be a Buddhist.

The Three Jewels

Buddha, Dhamma or Dharma and Sangha are known as the Three Jewels, the implication of this being that they are what Buddhists hold most dear in life. It is usual to make a commitment to them; this takes place in a formal ceremony which marks the intention to live a life that can be summarised in a verse found in the *Dhammapada*, a popular compilation of the Buddha's teaching.

Not to do evil
To cultivate good
To purify one's mind

The importance of this commitment is made clearer by contrasting these Three Jewels with what Buddhists understand to be the unhelpful influences in life, also termed the three poisons: greed or craving, which is sometimes also termed desire; hatred or aversion; and delusion or ignorance. The opposition of these triple formulations succinctly defines the Buddhist path. By inclining to the former, and seeking to avoid the influence of the latter, Buddhists understand the purpose of life.

The Three Refuges

Buddha, Dhamma (Dharma) and Sangha are also known as the Three Refuges. Refuge is not used in its negative sense of hiding away from something; rather, it means that which provides safety and the possibility of growth, that which you can put your trust in. For this reason, the formal recitation of the Three Jewels is described as 'going for refuge'. Although Buddhists of different persuasions would want to say a lot more about what this means and involves, we may begin here by saying that a Buddhist is one who has taken refuge in the Buddha, Dhamma and Sangha; from here, like the Buddha himself when he resolved to leave home in search of wisdom, he or she 'goes forth'.

Through the simple act of reciting this formula three times, one declares oneself a Buddhist.

> I go for refuge to the Buddha
> I go for refuge to the Dhamma
> I go for refuge to the Sangha.

The implication of this act is radically to reassess personal priorities and goals, as this passage written by a Japanese Buddhist teacher describes:

> Taking refuge is the first step on the Buddhist path to inner freedom, but it is not something new. We have been taking refuge all our lives, though mainly in external things, hoping to find security and happiness. Some of us take refuge in money, some in drugs. Some take refuge in food, in mountain-climbing or in sunny beaches. Most of us seek security and satisfaction in a relationship with a man or a woman. Throughout our lives we have drifted from one situation to the next, always in the expectation of final satisfaction. Our successive involvements may sometimes offer temporary relief but, in sober truth, seeking refuge in physical possessions and transient pleasures merely deepens our confusion rather than ending it.
>
> (Shunryu Suzuki, *Zen Mind, Beginners Mind*, Weatherhill, 1982, p 7)

Buddhist practice

What does this Buddhist way of life involve? First and foremost it is a practical path through life.

> It is only useful to you if it's practical. For me it is. I developed my meditation into an awareness and mindfulness and learned to do just what I was doing at any one time and nothing else. I find I pick up on things much quicker and am more open to other people. I have a better perspective on things and am more in touch with myself.
>
> In a business context, I've begun to investigate my motives

for doing the things I do in the business world. What do we really need? Food, shelter, clothes and medicine. That's about it. Of course I'm not perfect. I do lose it sometimes. I'm only human. But my practice decreases the percentage.

(Paul Queripel in *Target Magazine*, April 1988, p 12)

The Buddha's message stresses that speculation about the way things are is of little value. He spoke of investigating the human situation as a doctor investigates an illness, needing both diagnosis and cure. His teaching is a prescription. Speculation and discussion that does not focus on this is of no help. In a well-known passage he says that, if someone were struck by an arrow, he would not refuse to have it taken out until he knew who shot the arrow, whether he were married or not, what he looked like and so on: he would simply concentrate on removing it. In this way he indicated that he was not concerned with discussing the questions often regarded as of religious importance; for example, who created the world? how did it come into being? and so forth. These were considered by the Buddha as questions not tending to edification: what essentially matters is the here and now. Treading the Buddhist path should lead to a transformation in the self: a continuous refining of both thought and action, of the way we relate to others and to the world we live in: and finally of our self-understanding.

In the West, because of our lack of contact with traditionally Buddhist societies, erroneous views of Buddhism are prevalent. Buddhists are often thought to be other-worldly, concerned solely with a monastic life, retreating from society, looking inward and being unconcerned with everyday affairs. Buddhism is often believed to be a highly abstract philosophical system, academic and self-absorbing, of no value to the ordinary person. Such views would have bemused the Buddha, and possibly brought a wry smile to his face; however, they represent a barrier against understanding present-day Buddhists.

The Five Precepts (*Panca Sila*)

At the heart of Buddhist ethical practice are the Five Precepts. These are rules which identify the aspirations of a Buddhist. They are not commandments; rather, they are the minimum essential 'prescription' for treating the human condition, and an antidote to the three poisons: greed, aversion or hatred, and ignorance or delusion. They consist of the following undertakings:

1 I undertake to observe the precept to abstain from harming living beings.
2 I undertake to observe the precept to abstain from taking things not freely given.
3 I undertake to observe the precept to abstain from sexual misconduct.
4 I undertake to observe the precept to abstain from false speech.
5 I undertake to observe the precept to abstain from intoxicating drinks and drugs causing heedlessness.

> (adapted from *The Word of the Buddha*, Niyamatolika, The Buddhist Publication Society, 1971, p xii)

Of course, if carrying out these undertakings were as simple as it might seem, things would soon be well and good. However, the purpose of this commitment is, at least in part, to investigate what is *really* involved in leading this virtuous way of life. Thus, the more diligently you attempt to put the undertakings into practice, the more aware you become of their significance. This accords with the Buddha's exhortation that one should find things out for oneself. The cure can be prescribed by the doctor – but the patient must administer it and see if it works.

> Of whatever teachings you can assure yourself in this way, these teachings lead to calmness, not to neurotic passion, to mental freedom, not to bondage, to a decrease of worldly entanglements, not to an increase of them . . . of such teachings you may affirm with certainty, this is the Dhamma, this is the Ethical Life, this is the Master's Message.
>
> (*Vinaya, 11:10*, quoted in F.L.Woodward, *Some Sayings of the Buddha*, The Buddhist Society, London)

The Buddhist way of life is meant to consist in carrying a minimum of baggage, both material and spiritual. For this reason the Buddha's pronouncements can appear terse and austere, and imply a separation from society and a consequent introversion. However, if we apply the precepts in the way the Buddha intended, their function becomes clear. Here is the way one British Buddhist understands them:

> It's not a rule or a commandment. It's a promise I make to

myself. One thing I do each morning when I get up is to recite the simple Five Precepts: each morning I say them to myself – a bit loudly, but to myself: I take the view that I will not do such a thing. And then if I broke the promise I made in the morning, I'd feel a bit guilty, that I couldn't keep that promise today. But if I kept it, I'm quite happy that I did it. And then at night, just before I go to sleep, I repeat a stanza, which means that I have done such a thing, and I thank the Buddha for this doctrine, which I have learnt, and I have kept that side of it today.

(John Bowker, *Worlds of Faith*, BBC, 1983, p 133)

The Ten Precepts (*Dasa Sila*) and the Eight Precepts (*Attanga Sila*)

The Buddha laid down the Ten Precepts for *Samaneras* (those in training for the monastic life) and pious lay people unattached to families. They are the basis of the monastic code followed by *bhikkhus* (monks). The following are added to the basic Five Precepts:

6 I undertake to observe the precept to abstain from taking untimely meals.
7 I undertake to abstain from dancing, music, singing and watching grotesque mime.
8 I undertake to abstain from the use of garlands, perfumes and personal adornment.
9 I undertake to abstain from the use of high seats.
10 I undertake to abstain from accepting gold or silver.

(The Eight Precepts put numbers seven and eight together and omit the tenth.)

Lay Buddhists may undertake the Eight Precepts on festival days, but the Ten Precepts effectively determine the separation of monks from the rest of society as those who have taken up the mendicant life (relying on others for their physical and material needs), and become renunciants. The ideal behind the practice of the Ten Precepts is to be freed form all sensual entanglements. Thus the prohibitions involved prevent indulgence in food, entertainment, adornment, the seeking of status, personal importance and luxury, and the accumulation of wealth.

The significance of the precepts

It is worth investigating the significance of the precepts a little further. For example, taking the first precept, to abstain from harming any living being; this, at its most obvious level, would involve not killing another human being. In a more subtle way, it could involve making the effort to support, rather than ignore, the distress or suffering of another. Deciding not to do something for another's benefit is to harm him or her as much as deciding to do something that will obviously injure or kill. This is a precept that we can immediately relate to humans; however, our awareness may not so readily extend to other creatures. It may more easily extend to animals we are fond of, or find useful, than to those we do not value, or who threaten us and our well-being. The Buddha did not intend to instigate a long and ultimately unprofitable debate on this subject by advancing this precept as a guiding principle. For Buddhists, it is a matter of keeping the precept in mind when carrying out their day-to-day activities, whether they be cooking, driving, teaching or making important political decisions.

Thinking about the second precept, that of abstaining from things not given, we may interpret this as not stealing – in which case, to take another's property and not return it would be an obvious example; but to take something without permission would be another. To address the precept on a more subtle level might involve not invading someone's privacy, or their time to think or be alone. For thoughts, reflections and feelings are as much what one owns as material possessions.

When we start to consider the precepts as a whole, further considerations apply. Heedless actions suggest a lack of awareness of the influence of our own actions or presence upon others; when we relate this principle to a Buddhist virtue such as generosity, we become aware of the pervasiveness of this basic code. Whilst not infringing upon another's private life, it is important to be alert to ways in which our presence may be of value to them; this involves the dedication of time and effort, to the extent of relegating one's own concerns accordingly.

One British Buddhist puts it in this way:

It's quite possible to be British and Buddhist – though it's not easy, as Buddhist values are diametrically opposed to the 'me' and 'must get more' values apparently prevalent in today's society.

However, with awareness and care it is possible for Buddhist practice to flourish. For most of us mundane actions form the greater part of life – getting up in the morning, washing, dressing, going to work. These are the repeated experiences of my life and therefore offer a great opportunity for practice. Do I get up each morning bad-tempered? Do the soap I use, or the clothes I wear, exploit or abuse other living beings? Can the pollution created by my travelling to work be diminished? Constant awareness of how we use our bodies, speech and minds is Buddhist practice.

This practice develops compassion towards oneself and others. It brings joy as one sees its effects, and leads to peace as one minimises greed, hate and delusion.

> (quoted in C. Erricker, *Buddhism, E G Religions Source Book, The Guardian*, 1993, p 19)

In order to emphasise their value, a positive formulation of the precepts is sometimes used, which is recited as follows:

> With deeds of loving kindness, I purify my body.
> With open-handed generosity, I purify my body.
> With stillness, simplicity and contentment, I purify my body.
> With truthful communication, I purify my speech.
> With mindfulness, clear and radiant, I purify my mind.
> (*The FWBO Puja Book*, Windhorse Publications, 1984, p 18)

Mindfulness

Understanding the Buddhist view in the way described above leads us to consider how to achieve this refinement of attitude (or equanimity, to use a Buddhist term), whilst involved in the activity of our daily lives.

There is a story about a group of learned Buddhist monks who spent all their time in scholastic debate. As part of their banter they would often wonder, half-joking, half-seriously, which one of them would get enlightened first. Whenever this topic came up, the only thing they could all agree on was that it would not be Stupid, the illiterate monk who was capable only of sweeping the monastery floor and whom nobody has any time for. Of course, it was Stupid who got enlightened first. The jealous monks went to the Abbot. How come Stupid had got enlightened? Had he been overhearing their intellectual conversations? 'Not at all,' replied the Abbot, 'It's just that while he was sweeping the corners of the monastery he made sure he was also sweeping the corners of his mind.'

(Adrian Abbotts in C. Erricker and V. Barnett (eds), *World Religions in Education*, The Shap Working Party, 1989, p 11)

Remaining positive in outlook depends on not reacting negatively to events. However, the watchfulness and discipline required are obviously difficult to attain. The Buddha's teaching stressed as a supreme quality the cultivation of mindfulness; this involves an ability to watch over our own state of mind at the same time as observing the emotional fluctuations that occur in those around us. We cannot give to others without taking account of, and dealing with, the volatility present in our own nature. In simple terms, anger provokes anger, meanness provokes meanness, heedlessness provokes heedlessness. A crucial implication of the Buddha's teaching is that no-one is an island, but that by practising the Dhamma it is possible to influence the attitudes of those around us and of society at large. Indeed, the substance of this message goes still further. Not only human existence, but the destiny of the world, depend upon this taking place. It involves being in harmony with nature, and respect for all living things. Returning to the Indian context in which this teaching was first formulated, it goes beyond the span of our lives from birth to death, and determines our future rebirth. Buddhists consider that the capacity to progress to a more elevated spiritual and moral state has a fundamental effect on the evolution of the world. Adhering to the Dhamma will make the world a more harmonious place; the opposite will be true if the Dhamma is ignored. Equally, the individual will find the Dhamma easier or harder to follow as a consequence. Thus the microcosmic and macrocosmic understanding of individual action and cosmic evolution are intimately related. The capacity to be virtuous and to exhibit such qualities as generosity and loving kindness are steps on the path to becoming truly compassionate, which is one of the two supreme Buddhist attributes. The Buddha expressed this in one of his sermons to his first disciples.

Go forth on your journey, for the profit of the many, out of compassion for the world, for the welfare, the profit, the bliss of *devas* (gods) and mankind.

(*Vinaya, 1:21* quoted in F.L. Woodward, *Some Sayings of the Buddha*, The Buddhist Society, London, 1974).

Western Buddhist in meditation

Wisdom and compassion

Compassion (*karuna*) must be complemented by wisdom (*prajna*). The two are inseparable; they co-exist, and without the other neither is possible. The development of wisdom depends upon a more formal practice which, in western terms, is understood as meditation. In its earlier Indian context, it was a form of yoga. Yoga means to yoke or bind oneself, and here the notion of commitment is present once again. Without the discipline of a formal practice that allows understanding of the way in which one's own mind works, and development of the capacity for insight, the cultivation of compassion is inevitably diminished. One word for meditation that identifies its instrumental role is *bhavana* (mental or spiritual development); bhavana presumes that the latent capacity we have needs to be cultivated, in order for our full potential to be achieved. The purpose of this activity has been beautifully described by an influential twentieth-century meditation teacher in this way:

> Try to be mindful and let things take their natural course. Then your mind will become still in any surroundings, like a clear forest pool. All kinds of wonderful, rare animals will come to drink at the pool, and you will clearly see the nature of all things. You will see many strange and wonderful things come and go, but you will be still. This is the happiness of the Buddha.
>
> (Ajahn Chah, *A Still Forest Pool*, Kornfield and Breitner (eds), Quest Books, 1975)

This passage outlines succinctly the purpose of Buddhist meditation. Be calm (*samatha*) and you will become mindful. In this observant and detached state you will recognise what is actually happening and gain insight (*vipasanna*) into the way things truly are. From this arises a peace or happiness that allows a positive and virtuous response to others, regardless of the way in which you are treated. The result is attainment of both wisdom and compassion.

Another example can be found in the teaching of the Buddha, and his response to a situation that was far from the environment of academic debate and spiritual retreat. It emphasises the Buddhist concern to treat the root of the problem of human suffering, whilst not admitting that the events that cause such suffering are immediately avoidable.

Here the Buddha is helping the distressed mother of a dead child:

The story of Kisagotami

Kisagotami was born into a very poor family, and had the reputation of being frail and tiring easily. When she was old enough to be married she went to live with her husband's family. Because she had come from a poor home, they treated her without much respect until she gave birth to a son. The their attitude was quite different, and she was treated with both kindness and honour. Her situation was now a happy one, but this did not last for long. When her son was old enough to run about and play he became ill and died. Kisagotami was desolate. She had not only lost the child she loved, but also her respected position in her home. In her grief she picked up the body of her child and wandered from one house to another, asking for medicine for her son. The people who met her laughed and sneered. 'Whoever heard of medicine for the dead?' they said.

By now Kisagotami was almost driven out of her mind by her

sorrow. A wise man saw her wandering about and realised how much she needed help. He had heard some of the teaching of Gotama Buddha, and thought that he might be able to help her come to terms with her grief. He approached Kisagotami gently and told her that the Buddha was staying nearby and that he might have medicine for her son. 'Go and ask him,' he said.

Kisagotami went to find the Buddha and stood on the edge of the crowd, listening to him. When she had the chance, she called out to him, 'O, Exalted One, give me medicine for my son.'

Part of the Buddha's greatness lay in his skill in knowing how to help other people. He told her kindly to go to the city nearby and visit every house. 'Bring me some grains of mustard seed from every household in which no-one has ever died.'

Kisagotami was delighted. Here was someone who took her seriously. She went to the city, knocked on the first house and asked for some grains of mustard seed from the householder, if no-one had ever died there. The householder told her with great sadness that he had recently lost his wife. Kisagotami listened to his story with growing sympathy, understanding his grief from her own. She eventually moved on, but found that in every house there was a story of sickness, old age and death. Her own grief seemed different now that she shared that of others, and she realised that the Buddha had known when he sent her out that she would find that her predicament was the common experience of human beings. Death is the law common to all that lives. She now took the body of her dear little son to the cremation ground and let it be cremated, fully realising that all is impermanent.

Kisagotami then returned to Gotama Buddha. He asked her whether she had brought him the grains of mustard seed. She told him what had happened, and what she had realised. She then asked him to accept her as his follower and to teach her more about the nature of reality and the path to understanding.

(taken from Peggy Morgan, *Buddhist Stories*, Private Publication from the author at Westminster College, Oxford OX2 9AT, p 22)

Though wisdom and compassion are the quintessential aspirations of all Buddhists, they are equally aware that they are not immediately attainable, and may take many lifetimes to achieve; in fact they represent Buddhahood itself. Therefore it is important to focus on the task in hand, rather than continually to attempt to peer over the horizon. The Dalai Lama, a revered figure in the Buddhist world who attracts the devotion and respect of Tibetan and Western Buddhists alike, is very adept at expressing Buddhist concerns in a much more down-to-earth way.

> Simplicity is important for happiness. Having few desires, feeling satisfied with what you have is vital. Many are making a great effort to control external things – like arms control. But without being able to control inner things, how can you control external arms? Real arms control is to control anger.
>
> Now I am talking as a human being, not as a Buddhist. This I think is most important, because ideology and religion are for human beings, not the other way round. They are secondary. Emphasis should be on humanity.
>
> My religion is very simple – my religion is kindness.
>
> There is so much effort spent on external matters, like space travel. But there is still quite a big area of inner space left to explore. And it's not so expensive!
>
> People think patience is weakness. But I think not. Anger comes from fear, and fear from weakness. So, if you have strength then you have more courage. This is where patience comes from.
>
> Deep down we must have real affection for each other, a clear recognition of our shared humanity. At the same time, we must accept all ideologies and systems as a means of solving humanity's problems.
>
> (*The Dalai Lama: Kindness, Clarity and Insight*, quoted in *Resurgence*, Issue 123, July/August 1987, p 23)

Skilfulness

We have noted that following the precepts, and developing insight through meditation, are two basic and interconnected practices of the Buddhist life, and that through these Buddhists seek to become wiser and more compassionate. There is a third element that plays a necessary part in this development. Skilfulness, or skill in means, (*upaya*) was a supreme quality of the Buddha. As a teacher he was not giving information which, once received, could immediately be understood. In fact, one of the most crucial moments in the Buddha's life came when, after achieving enlightenment (*bhodi*) or awakening, he was daunted by the prospect of trying to convey what he now knew to any-one. He perceived that humans were too caught up in worldly attach-ments to hear and understand that happiness lay beyond worldly con-cerns, and that suffering was a result of living in ignorance of this knowledge. His resolve changed, and his teaching career began only when, in the mythological but highly poetic way in which this event is conveyed in the Buddhist scriptures, the god Brahma came to the Buddha and exhorted him, out of compassion for the world, to share his wisdom because, 'there are beings with a little dust in their eyes who, not hearing the Dharma, are decaying.'

For Buddhists, this event, along with the Buddha's first sermon in the Deer Park at Benares, is of seminal importance. This is the point at which the Buddhist tradition began, with the Buddha's resolve to teach the Dhamma, and it illustrates why Buddhists often refer to themselves as 'followers of the Dhamma' rather than as Buddhists or followers of the Buddha.

Only because the Buddha taught it did the Dhamma appear in the world, and only because of the Buddha's supreme skilfulness in the way he taught – by word and deed – was it possible for others to understand and follow the Dhamma themselves. This skilfulness is therefore also a quality to which Buddhists aspire, and which they value highly. Without it the Dhamma would not be passed on.

We have already read one example of the Buddha's skilfulness in addressing the plight of Kisagotami. Another example of skilfulness is revealed in this Zen story, called *The Muddy Road*.

> Two monks were walking down a muddy road, and came across a young woman trying to cross it but unable to avoid a large pool of water. The first monk was inclined just to walk on. The sec-ond promptly helped the woman by lifting her up and carrying her across. Following this incident the two monks walked on, but there was obvious tension between them. After a while the first monk, unable to contain his anger any longer, remonstrat-ed with the second, saying, 'You know it is against our vows to touch a woman, why did you lift her up and carry her?' The sec-ond monk replied 'I may have carried her back there but you are still carrying her and you haven't yet let her go.'
>
> (P. Reps, *Zen Flesh, Zen Bones*, Penguin, 1971, p 28)

This ability to let go is an example of skilfulness. The first monk still harboured his latent desire in his mind. The second was aware that eradicating such a desire was more important than just following the monks' rule of not touching women. The first monk had forgotten what the rule was there for. The story illustrates that skilfulness (or lack of it) relates to the motivation behind the act, whether or not it does harm to oneself or the world. The skilfulness required to let go of desire is described in a very practical fashion by this teacher:

> To be aware, we have to use skilful means . . . The obsession of 'letting go' is a skilful one – as you repeat this over and over, whenever a thought arises, you are aware of its arising. You keep letting go of whatever moves – but if it doesn't go, don't try to force it. This 'letting go' practice is a way of clearing the mind of its obsessions and negativity; use it gently, but with resolution. Meditation is a skilful means of letting go, of deliberately emptying out the mind so we can see the purity of the mind – cleaning it out so we can put the right things in it.
>
> You respect your mind, so you are more careful what you put in it. If you have a nice house, you don't go out and pick up all the filth from the street and bring it in; you bring in things that will enhance it and make it a refreshing and delightful place.
>
> (Ajahn Sumedo, Cittaviveka: *Teachings from the Silent Mind*, Amaravati Publications, 1992, p 31)

This pinpoints what really matters to Buddhists: the purity of the mind uncluttered by greed and self-concern, which leads to compassionate activity in the world.

Awakening

The Buddha's great achievement was to attain enlightenment or *Nirvana* (*Nibbana*). He is said to have attained Nirvana under a pipal tree in Bodh-Gaya, in north-east India. (In Buddhist tradition, this tree is now named after his achievement and called a *Bodhi* (enlightenment) tree. This event provides the inspiration for all Buddhists. The term, 'awakening', perhaps explains the significance of this event in a more accessible way. It is an awakening to the way things truly are, and an extinguishing of the ignorance that fetters us to continual rebirth in the realm of *samsara*, which we can translate as motivation by desire, ignorance and aversion. Nirvana literally means 'to extinguish'.

Nirvana is not a place, in geographical terms, other than where we are. It is not a heaven, in the other-worldly sense of the term. But it *is* a recognition that our potential is not fulfilled by our day to day concern for advancement or survival, nor is it denied by our ultimate fear of extinction or death. The Buddha's teaching is, as one Zen saying puts it, like a finger pointing at the moon. To mistake the teaching for the truth is to misunderstand the nature of the journey. The teaching is a vehicle, and the Buddha told a parable to this effect:

'Using the figure of a raft, brethren, will I teach you the Dhamma as something to leave behind, not to take with you. Do you listen to it. Apply your minds. I will speak.

'Just as a man, brethren, who has started on a long journey sees before him a great stretch of water, on this side full of doubts and fears, on the further side safe and free from fears . . . Then he thinks thus: . . . "How now if I were to gather together grass, sticks and branches, and leaves, bind them into a raft, and resting on that raft paddle with hands and feet and so come safe to the further shore?"

'Then brethren, that man gathers together sticks . . . and comes to the further shore. When he has crossed over and come to the other side he thinks thus: "This raft has been of great use to me. Resting on this raft and paddling with hand and foot I have come to the further shore. Suppose now I were to set this raft on my head or lift it on to my shoulders and go my ways?"

'Now what think ye, brethren? Would that man in so doing have finished with that raft?'

'Surely not, Lord.'

'Doing what then, brethren, would that man have finished with that raft? Herein, brethren, that man who has crossed and gone to the further shore should think thus: "This raft has been of great use to me. Resting on it I have crossed to the further shore. Suppose now I haul it up on the shore or sink it in the water and go my ways!" By so doing, brethren, that man would have finished with that raft.

'Figuratively, then, Nirvana is that 'further shore' of full realisation.

Even so, brethren, using the figure of a raft have I shown you the Dhamma, as something to leave behind, not to take with you. Thus, brethren, understanding the figure of the raft, ye must leave behind righteous ways, not to speak of unrighteous ways.'

(Majjhima Nikaya 1, 134, quoted in F.L. Woodward, *Some Sayings of the Buddha*, The Buddhist Society, London, 1974)

2
THE LIFE OF
THE BUDDHA

The Buddha's significance

The word 'Buddha' is a title given by his followers to the teacher Siddhartha Gautama (Siddhatta Gotama), who lived in India 2,500 years ago. We might well ask what relevance such a figure and his life can have for us today. Our pursuit of progress in the modern world suggests that we constantly gain more knowledge as time goes by. Yet we only have to reflect on the weight of human suffering that remains and re-emerges throughout human history (and is just as prevalent, if not more so, in the twentieth century) to realise there are certain problems that our accumulated knowledge simply cannot address. More sophisticated technology and scientific advances do not get to the root of the problem of human conflict and suffering. More efficient communication in a technological sense is not to be equated with better communication between human beings. Ultimately, some problems just will not go away, however hard we address them. Such problems can be understood as matters of the heart as well as of the mind. We cannot solve them with logic alone, by creating a more comfortable material life for ourselves, or even by furthering our medical knowledge and skill. When we understand that scientific and technological achievement is not a panacea for all ills, we can comprehend the persistence of ancient wisdoms in the context of searching for answers to apparently insoluble human dilemmas; we also see what it is about the Buddha that makes him as fascinating a figure in today's world as he was in the far-off Indian culture within which he lived. Here are two personal reflections that give us some clues to his importance.

Among the ruins of Anuradhapura, the ancient capital of Sri Lanka, there rests alone on a pedestal above the grass a seated image of the Buddha in stone, slightly larger than life. The statue is conventional, probably more than a thousand years old, of a type found throughout Buddhist Asia. The legs are folded in meditation, the hands laid one upon the other in the lap. Buddhists hold that it was in this posture, seated beneath a tree more than 2500 years ago, that the Buddha was awakened, attaining decisive knowledge of the human condition and the unshakeable certainty that he was released from its suffering.

In its excellence, however, the Anuradhapura image is far from conventional. The back and head are disciplined and upright; but the arms are relaxed and the face reposes in tranquility. The figure seems intelligent and serene, wed perfectly to the unmoving granite. Standing before it an elderly English socialist told me that in the whole mess of human history this at least – the statue and all it stands for – was something of which we could be proud. He said that he had no use for religion, but that he felt he had unknowingly been a follower of the Buddha all along.

(M. Carrithers, *The Buddha*), Oxford University Press, 1983, p 1)

What have I learnt from the masters I have listened to, the philosophers I have read, the societies I have investigated, and that very science in which the West takes such pride? Simply a fragmentary lesson or two which, if laid end to end, would add up to the meditations of the Sage at the foot of his tree.

(ibid., pp 1–2)

Buddhists, of course, are much more precise about his relevance and the way in which his life unfolded. This is illustrated, as follows, according to Buddhist tradition.

The Four Sights

Siddhartha was born into comparative privilege, the son of a chief (king or raja) of the Sakya people of north-eastern India (in present-day Nepal). His early life equipped him for government and the inheritance of his father's position. However, his education and social standing also allowed him a degree of choice as to his future; and, so the narrative tells, his father was well aware of this possibility. The traditional story describes how Queen Mahamaya, the wife of King Suddhodama and Siddhartha's mother, was troubled by a dream which was interpreted to mean that she was to have a son who would one day become either a king or a *sadhu* (a holy man who has renounced worldly things). When Siddhartha was born, and throughout his childhood and adolescence, the king was anxious that he should choose the former vocation, and so organised his life to ensure, as far as possible, that this would occur. He was surrounded by beautiful things and kept within the palace grounds. He was married to the beautiful Princess Yasodhara, who then gave birth to their son. The combination of a pleasant, fulfilling life, with the responsibility of a family, was thought to prepare the young prince for his inheritance – socially and psychologically – and his education also reflected this. The king's hope was shattered by what, in Buddhist tradition, is called the Four Sights. Siddhartha grew restless of his palace life, and sought to know of the world outside. He directed his charioteer to take him out into the world beyond the confines of the palace, and encountered experiences that had an abiding effect and shaped his future life. The first time he ventured beyond the palace precincts he saw an old man, and questioned his companion as to why he was so bent and frail. Siddhartha was struck by the answer he was given: that this was the eventual lot of all human beings, including himself. It was a natural and unavoidable event. His response was, 'What is the use of this youth, vitality and strength, if it all ends in this?'

The second sight, on his next excursion beyond the palace, was of a sick person. Again, he was struck by the fact that disease and malady afflict even the strongest and healthiest of individuals and, more importantly, that there is no way of anyone preventing it.

The third sight was of a corpse being carried to the cremation ground on a stretcher. This was, and still is, a common sight in India, where the dead are not hidden from the public eye by coffins or hearses, and where the burning of the dead is open to public view, most conspicuously on the *ghats* beside rivers, for example at Varanasi beside the Ganges. Again, what the charioteer understood to be an everyday event and a typical aspect of life stunned Siddhartha. What struck him most forcibly was the lack of control and direction people ultimately have over their own life and destiny: you don't want to grow old but you can't help it. You don't want to fall sick but you can't ensure against it. Death is unavoidable and yet it makes a nonsense of living.

Where is the meaning and purpose in all this? The agonised questioning of Siddhartha is contrasted, in the story, with the unquestioning acceptance of this state of affairs betrayed by Khanna, his charioteer. Siddhartha awoke to the true nature of being in this world, to the state of samsara, characterised by old age, sickness, death and continual becoming. It was pointless nonsense to live with the acceptance that there is nothing humans can do to alter this state of affairs, whatever other knowledge and sophistication they may achieve. For him, perhaps the most striking discovery of these ventures into the outside world was that humans accept this as their lot, as natural.

Siddhartha's reaction to the first three sights exemplifies the Buddhist starting-point: seeing to the heart of the matter. What happens after that, in terms of the decisions one makes and the life one leads, is rooted in the understanding that this is the fundamental problem that must be addressed. Similarly, therefore, we can appreciate that to see that life is characterised by suffering, but not to act upon that awareness, is a wholly 'un-Buddhist' attitude. Such pessimism, or fatalism, is completely contrary to Buddhist understanding. Once the problem has been identified, one is immediately committed to doing something about it. The retrospective telling of the Buddha's journey to enlightenment reveals that, behind the serene smile and composed form of later Buddha images, lies a story of inner struggle revealed in the narratives of the Buddha's life. The story of the Four Sights indicates the resolve of a restless heart to pursue resolutely an uncompromised goal. What is told as four brief excursions into a matter-of-fact and everyday world highlights the significance, for Buddhists, of waking up to the reality that the world we take as given and ordinary is really a fantastic state of affairs. It is only by dwelling on this, and by resolving to transform our own understanding of what it means to take full advantage of a human life, that we can fulfill our human potential.

For Siddhartha, the fourth sight was the inspiration to this end. This fourth sight was of a sadhu, or holy man, walking the streets with his alms bowl. This is a relatively common sight in Indian life. It was, and is, the alternative way of life to that of the householder, the one who has fulfilled his duty of bringing up a family and following a traditional occupation. Such a person was understood as a mendicant, one who has given up wealth and material gain by virtue of relying on others for his basic sustenance, shelter and livelihood. In contrast to the householder, the sadhu is a 'wandering one' (*anagarika*) who has acknowledged that this ordinary world of change and suffering (called the realm of samsara) is one in which no home, in the spiritual sense, can be found. To put it bluntly, the riddle of existence and human destiny cannot be resolved simply by pursuing one's social duties.

This was the dilemma that confronted Siddhartha. To pursue the life of the sadhu, everything had to be given up: his expected future career, his marriage and family, his security in the life of the palace and his fulfilment of parental expectations. We have no knowledge of how he came to resolve this dilemma, but he did; without that Buddhism would not have come into being.

Going forth

The stories tell how, on the night of a full moon, Siddhartha bade farewell to his sleeping wife and child. He rode to the edge of the Sakya kingdom, divested himself of his clothes, long hair and beard, and resolved to go forth as a wandering one. This event is understood in Buddhist terms as Siddhartha's 'going forth': the moment of commitment to a renunciant's life and the beginning of his search, his new career. It was not an interim rite of passage between an adolescent life and adulthood responsibilities that could be shelved for a while. Nor was it the irresponsibly conceived act of an impetuous young man. It was a resolute change of direction that established a tradition whose impact would last for millennia. Should we wish to criticise such an act we should also have to take into account its positive consequences. This is why, for Buddhists everywhere, commitment is fundamental.

However, this is not to say that it entails the same social consequences. In the history of Buddhist tradition it is true that joining the Sangha has often entailed leaving behind family life for a monastic one. For this reason, monks and monastic life have always been at the centre of traditional Buddhist societies. Taking up the monastic life is seen as imitating the commitment of Siddartha in his going forth to a mendicant's existence. Becoming a monk is to become a mendicant. However, Buddhism has also always taken into account the need to adapt its form to different cultural and social circumstances. It has been able to do this because the idea of commitment is not fundamentally a matter of changing one's status in society, but of adapting one's outlook and goals.

Buddhist understanding of the distinction between the outer form and inner resolution has been highlighted (especially in the West today), such that there are Buddhist groups who understand renunciation and commitment to the Buddhist tradition to be a way of living within conventional society with different codes and aspirations, rather than an opting-out of the given social order. This amounts in part to an understanding of the difference between the Indian society of the Buddha's day and our own. Monasticism was an obvious route for the development of the Buddhist ideal of community, given the options open to spiritual searchers in the Buddha's time. Today it represents something different. The question of adaptation versus the appropriate vehicle for the life lived in pursuit of the truth (dharma) has always been a live issue, but no more so than now. What has always been important is the Buddhist notion of a spiritual community, and this is what the term *sangha* denotes.

However, this takes us beyond the point which Siddartha had reached in his own journey. After leaving home, he was confronted with the alternatives available to him in Indian society. Foremost among these were the ascetic practices of yogis who, through austerity and denial of physical nourishment, sought to realise their spiritual aspirations. Subjugation of the flesh was for them a necessary prerequisite to spiritual advancement. (This is not just a matter of historical interest since, in India at least, it is still practised.) Unlike in the West, where the notion of austerity belongs more to the past, as redundant as the monastic life, in India the large number of sadhus who devote themselves to this cause can be witnessed readily at dawn on the banks of the Ganges, and at the great pilgrimage festivals, such as Kumb Mela in Allahabad, which they attend.

Self-mortification

Siddartha pursued the path of self-mortification for six years, limiting his food and sleep, not washing and living naked, or, in the sky-clad state, as it was known. He gained a reputation amongst fellow ascetics, gathering disciples and companions. His fame, it is said, spread like the sound of a great gong in the canopy of the sky. Though he achieved states of higher consciousness and greater awareness, he finally gave up these practices because he came to the conclusion that they did not lead to the realisation of the truth (the cessation of suffering). He started eating again, and his followers and companions deserted him. He continued to travel alone, seeking out other teachers, but finally became disillusioned by all their practices. He eventually reached a spot where he resolved to remain until he achieved enlightenment. This is now a well-known moment, both in Buddhist tradition and in world history. Beneath the shade of a great pipal tree, later named after this event as a Bodhi (enlightenment) tree, beside a river, he resolved, 'I will not rise from this spot until I am enlightened. Flesh may wither away, blood may dry up, but until I gain enlightenment I shall not move from this seat.'

The Buddha in meditation.

The enlightenment

It is not easy to imagine what occurred in the mind of one sitting so motionless. It seems ironic that such a great event – the rediscovery of truth – should outwardly be so uneventful. But it is indicative of the character of Buddhism that it should be so: truth is found in silence and stillness rather than activity. He sat there in a meditative state, gaining greater concentration and control of his mind. This state of purification was not achieved instantly, but was the result of all the training he had undertaken since leaving home. It involved overcoming the mental hindrances that disrupt and unbalance the mind.

These are graphically described in Buddhist writings as the attacks of Yama, the Lord of Death, who recognised the significance of the Buddha's quest and opposed it with all his power. We can be sure that this was not a serene and easily-accomplished endeavour, but called on all the Buddha's resolve and skill. All doubt, indecision and compromise had to be exposed, rather like a tortuous inner struggle in which this was the final battle. We are told that on the night of the full moon of Wesak (the month of May in the western calendar), the Buddha fixed his mind on the morning star as it was rising, and the moment of full enlightenment occurred.

Essentially, Siddartha became the Buddha at this point; when he eradicated all ignorance, and saw things for exactly what they were with crystal clarity. If we try and imagine what this could be like, we might think of times when, in trying to understand apparently complex, insoluble problems, we have hit on an instant when answers revealed themselves so obviously that it was as though we had previously missed what was right before our eyes. Moments when we have said, 'Of course, how could I have been so blind!' This helps us to understand why the event is referred to as 'The Great Awakening', and why the term 'letting go' is so often used by Buddhists to indicate the nature of such wisdom.

The idea of striving for the truth does not really communicate the whole nature of Siddhartha's achievement. It is as though the truth has been there all the time, but we have not had the capacity to realise it. It was this capacity that Siddartha developed and finally fulfilled. This was the end of Siddhartha's original search but, like all ends, it created a new beginning. As the Buddha, the fully enlightened one, Siddhartha was not the same person he had previously understood himself to be. The wisdom and compassion conferred on him by this event also registered new responsibilities. He who knows is the only one who can make the truth known to others.

The practical significance of truth is what constitutes its ultimate value. It is conquest over death. The individual is freed from the fetters of this life. No longer is he or she condemned to constant rebirth and the dis-ease that results from this. From a Buddhist point of view, this does not mean that we are changed into other beings, gods or angels; rather, we have realised our true nature, our complete potential. (Were this not the case, the Buddha's achievement would amount to a comfort or solace, a way of living well within the prison-house of existence – but nothing more). In this respect, the Buddha becomes a unique historical figure, because his achievement is to present a spiritual goal achievable without the aid of a god. This is not to say that Buddha or Buddhists are necessarily antagonistic towards theistic belief, but that it is not seen as either skilful or helpful to look to a god to solve the riddle of human existence.

Turning the wheel of the Dharma

The difficulty of disclosing this truth to others was something that did not immediately resolve itself for the Buddha. As we have seen, he was initially unsure that it could be comprehended by anyone, but the Buddha's teaching career began with his sermon at Sarnath, where he encountered his former companions and preached the Dharma for the first time. The distance from Bodh Gaya, the place of his enlightenment, to Sarnath, is one hundred miles, and we can only speculate on what went through his mind while he made the journey. However, when he met his first audience, they were struck by his overall disposition, which radiated those virtues held in high esteem by Buddhists. The confidence and equanimity with which he encountered them were a prelude to the acceptance of his teaching, and drew to him the community that was to grow up around him.

It was not just what the Buddha had to say, but the confidence he inspired in those whom he addressed, that won over his audience. At first, his five former companions greeted him with scepticism, for he was that same Gotama who had given up the path of ascetic practice. However, struck by his authority, they received him back into their company and subsequently became his followers. One writer relates the event as follows:

> Upon this the Buddha told them of his experience and claimed recognition of his enlightenment. The monks were once more sceptical. They failed to use the new and higher title of Tathagatha (one who has gone beyond), which implies the status

of Buddhahood, and which the narrative makes the Buddha claim for himself. After all, they argued, Gotama had not arrived at this exalted knowledge when he had practised austerities, so why should they believe that he had done so when he reverted to ordinary ways of living? The Buddha retorted that a Tathagata was not one who had reverted to a life of abundance, giving up the quest for self-mastery. And he repeated his claim to have reached perfect enlightenment and to have found 'the deathless'. The other monks should hear his teaching, and they too would arrive at the goal which they sought when they first left home. Still the monks demurred, and as the narrative gives human truth in story form, the argument is repeated three times. Finally the Buddha makes them admit that he had never talked in such a way before, and that he therefore really did have something to say. So they decided to hear him out. Although by this time he had already trodden quite a few miles and spoken not a few thoughts, we now come to what is usually known as the Buddha's first teaching, or more picturesquely, the first rolling of the wheel of the Dhamma.

(M. Pye, *The Buddha*, Duckworth, 1979, p 41)

Such stories as these also remind us that the Buddha's teaching career was not just a matter of preaching to a willing audience, but that the complex quality of skilfulness (upaya) was an essential ingredient for winning over committed individuals (often of great integrity), to an acknowledgement of his claims, which are presented in the formulation of his teachings. There is no doubt that the Buddha was a charismatic figure, but his charisma was understood as radiating not from cleverness or intellectual status (which would have attracted only those with an inclination towards such attributes), but from a deep knowledge that went beyond aspects of his personality.

The mission

The Buddha practised the life of an itinerant preacher, roaming across north-eastern India for the remainder of his life, from his enlightenment at the age of thirty-five. Following climatic conditions, the pattern he established was to wander from place to place for nine months of the year, and take shelter during the three-month monsoon period; these three months became established as a time of retreat and remain so for some monastic Buddhist communities today.

Taking one meal a day, whenever he came to a village, he established the practice of standing at the villagers' doors silently with his alms bowl; once he had collected sufficient food, he would retire to a mango grove on the outskirts of a village to eat. After his meal, villagers would gather round to hear him teach. In this way his following increased, drawn from different strata in the caste-orientated Indian society. From these occasions are drawn various conversations which have entered into the Buddhist scripture. The story of Kisagotami is one such, but there are others, which reflect the character of the Buddha's teaching, the people whom he met, and their response to him. Some of these accounts may well have been elevated to mythology, but they provide us with some valuable information. One of the first of the Buddha's village meetings is related in this story:

Dona and the Buddha

Journeying along the high road, the Buddha met a man called Dona. Dona was a brahmin, and skilled in the science of bodily signs. Seeing on the Buddha's footprints the mark of a thousand-spoked wheel, he followed in his track along the road until he eventually caught up with the Buddha, who was sitting beneath a tree. As the Buddha was fresh from his Enlightenment, there was a radiance about his whole being. We are told it was as though a light shone from his face – he was happy, serene, joyful. Dona was very impressed by his appearance, and he seems to have felt that this wasn't an ordinary human being, perhaps not a human being at all. Drawing nearer, he came straight to the point, as the custom is in India where religious matters are concerned. He said, 'Who are you?'

Now the ancient Indians believed that the universe is stratified into various levels of existence, that there are not just human beings and animals, as we believe, but gods, and ghosts, and yaksas, and gandharvas, and all sorts of other mythological beings, inhabiting a multi-storey universe, the human plane being just one storey out of many. So Dona asked 'Are you a yaksa?' (a yaksa being a rather terrifying sublime spirit living in the forest). But the Buddha said 'No'. Just 'No'. So Dona tries again. 'Are you a gandharva?' (a sort of celestial musician, a beautiful singing angel-like figure). Once again the Buddha said 'No', and again Dona asked 'Well, then, are you a deva?' (a god, a divine being, a sort of archangel). 'No'. Upon this Dona thought, 'That's strange, he must be a human being after all!' And he asked him that too, but yet again the Buddha said 'No'. By this time Dona was thoroughly perplexed, so he demanded 'If you are not any of these things, then who are you?' The Buddha replied, 'Those mental conditionings on account of which I might have been described as a yaksa or a gandharva, as a deva or a human being, all those conditionings have been destroyed by me. Therefore I am a Buddha.'

(Ven. Sangharakshita, *A Guide to the Buddhist Path*,
Windhorse Publications, 1990, pp 36–37)

What is evident from this story is that the Buddha's knowledge and experience challenged the world view of his own culture, and of succeeding cultures up to the present day. It was not that he offered an understanding of the world and our experience within it, for that complemented what we already know. Rather he turned our understanding upside-down, such that it had to be fundamentally changed to accommodate his teaching. As with all the great religious teachers, a new way of looking at the world and reflecting on the human condition was being offered. If this hadn't been the case, the Buddhist tradition would never have developed in its own unique and independent way.

The story also suggests that it is not enough to know about the Buddha and his teachings because his claims, as with all great religious teachers, confront our own self-awareness. What is being questioned is not whether we need to know more, but whether our understanding is fundamentally ignorant – without real knowledge. This amounts to a confrontation of view, without which the Buddha would not have gained so many followers, nor established a lasting tradition. It is a matter of commitment that involves the whole person, rather than simply adding to individual personal philosophy. For this reason it is not appropriate to regard the Buddha simply as an ancient philosopher, in the manner of Plato or Aristotle. One could investigate the Buddha's teaching as a philosophy, but that would not amount to knowledge in the Buddhist sense because it does not confer what Buddhists call 'right view'. Only by applying his

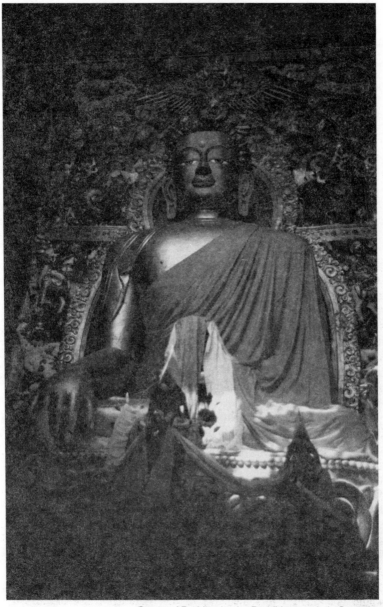

Statue of Buddha (at the Buddhist temple in Sarnath)

teachings in practice does realisation arise; then the truth is confirmed and self-transformation occurs.

The Buddha was by no means uniformly successful in his encounters. Another early meeting was with the wandering ascetic Upaka, described as an *ajiveka* (who are sometimes known as naked ascetics, renowned for their austerity).

Upaka and the Buddha

Upaka met the Buddha on the road near Bodh Gaya and noticed that he seemed particularly clear of complexion. He greeted him respectfully and asked him, in the way such travellers did, who his teacher was or what his Dhamma was. The Buddha replied in words of incomparable self-assurance that he was victorious, omniscient, teacher-less and unequalled among gods and men. He alone was completely enlightened. He had attained nirvana. Upaka replied, perhaps ironically, that he certainly sounded as if he had conquered 'the unending'; with which the Buddha did not hesitate to agree. Upaka was unconvinced. 'That may be so', he said, and off he went down another road, shaking his head.

(Michael Pye: *The Buddha*, Duckworth, 1979, p 40)

This helps us to understand that in the world of his time there were others who belonged to already established spiritual traditions sharing the same aspirations as the Buddha had done. It was by no means easy to convince such determined searchers that he had already achieved what they were still looking for. Indeed it is apparent that today also such scepticism acts as an important antidote to naïve commitment or 'blind faith'. It was an important aspect of the Buddha's teachings that you had to commit yourself to the practice, as was mentioned in Chapter 1. It was this recognition in fact that determined the way in which the Buddha formulated his discourses; on the basis that unless they addressed the fundamental message he had to convey – the overcoming of suffering – and unless their truth was discernible through application, they were of no recognisable value.

The growth of the sangha

Starting with the five former companions, the Buddha's followers grew into an Order of Monks (the *Bhikkhu Sangha*) which drew in lay people to the mendicant life. As the missionary preaching of the order spread, so lay people 'went for refuge' to the Buddha, without renouncing their status as householders, and the lay community developed. This balance between monastic and lay life in the Sangha was one of the main features of the Buddha's mission during his teaching career, which spanned forty years. It was the blueprint for harmony and balance in the social order that transformed the movement, from its initial character as a mendicant group, into an influential Indian tradition that, centuries later, was to convert the Emperor Ashoka, who sought to rule the sub-continent according to Buddhist principles.

Women had been ordained as members of the Order, though the Buddha's attitude had been ambiguous; he accepted them with some reluctance and warned monks of the need to be vigilant in their presence. In answer to his disciple Ananda's question, asking how monks should behave in the presence of women, he is recorded as saying, 'No talking' and, 'Keep wide awake'. This may be ascribed to his belief that attachment to women was a major obstacle in the attainment of nirvana; whatever the reason, such sayings should be put in the context of the whole code of monastic discipline (*vinaya*) that the Buddha laid down.

Paranirvana

The Buddha's death, in his old age, was said to be by food-poisoning, from having inadvertently eaten unwholesome mushrooms, truffles or pork, which had been offered to him. It is said that he passed away in a state of meditation, reclining on his right side, his head supported by his hand. This posture has been recorded in Buddhist iconography, and is understood as the Buddha's passing into *Paranirvana* – Nirvana without remainder; a state in which he was no longer subject to rebirth. This occurred in the woodlands outside the town of Kusinara. He appointed no successor and, it seems, he wished the Sangha to remain a relatively non-hierarchical organisation. Among his last words were these to Ananda, who, aware of the imminent death of the Buddha, was leaning against the door-frame weeping. The Buddha called Ananda to him, saying 'do not mourn, do not weep.

Haven't I told you that we are separated, parted, cut off from everything dear and beloved? . . . You have served me long with love, helpfully, gladly, sincerely and without reserve, in body, word and thought. You have done well by yourself, Ananda. Keep trying and you will soon be liberated.'

3

THE BUDDHA'S
TEACHING

Thus have I heard. The Blessed One was once living in the Deer
Park at Isipatana (the Resort of Seers) near Varanasi (Benares).
There he addressed the group of five bhikkhus.

This is the beginning of what is referred to as the first discourse
(*darsana*) of the Buddha, as it appears in the collected writings of the
Buddhist canon, the *suttas* (*sutras*). Sutta means thread, and this
term is used to express the connected ideas that constitute a discourse of the Buddha. In this case we are listening to the way in
which the Buddha formulated his basic understanding of the human
condition, and expounded it to those who first listened, his original
companions, who were to become his bhikkus (monks or followers).

This teaching addresses the Four Noble Truths and the Middle
Way – the crux of the Buddha's teaching pared down to the single
concept of *dukkha* (suffering or 'unsatisfactoriness'), why it is the
fundamental aspect of the human condition, and how it can be overcome. It relates to the Buddha's own life and experiences.

> Bhikkhus, these two extremes ought not to be practised by one
> who has gone forth from the household life. What are the two?
> There is devotion to the indulgence of sense-pleasures, which is
> low, common, the way of ordinary people, unworthy and unprof-
> itable; and there is devotion to self-mortification, which is
> painful, unworthy and unprofitable.
>
> (W. Rahula: *What the Buddha Taught*,
> Gordon Fraser, 1982 p 92)

The Buddha knew about indulgence in sensual pleasures from his life in the palace, and about self-mortification from his early renunciant experiences; and by reflecting on these he developed the teaching of the Middle Way, which leads to 'vision, knowledge, calm, insight, enlightenment, Nibbana'.

The Middle Way is also the fourth of the Noble Truths that the Buddha expounded. To understand this we must first look at the three propositions that lead up to it, which resulted in his exposition of the Buddhist path, and which, together with the fourth, the Middle Way, constitute the Four Noble Truths:

1 Dukkha, disease or suffering
2 Samudaya, the arising or origin of dukkha
3 Nirodha, the cessation of dukkha
4 Magga, the way leading to the cessation of dukkha

The first Noble Truth:
all is suffering (*Dukkha*)

It is very difficult to translate the term dukkha accurately. One word, such as suffering, is insufficient and misleading. It is not a purely philosophical term, and it would be wrong to treat it in that way. Suffering is one meaning ascribed to it, but this suggests a pessimistic view, somehow stressing the bad things and ignoring the good that happens in the course of human experience. It is necessary to understand that *experience* is the key word here. What the Buddha is pointing to is the weight of understanding brought about by reflecting on the totality of a life lived, not simply by weighing its pros and cons. Other words that help to elucidate its meaning are dis-ease, imperfection and inadequacy. It is not that life does not have its happy moments as well as the unhappy ones, but that the sum total of human experience is inadequate or imperfect. It is not all one might hope for or expect. Such expectation or hope is not a matter of false optimism or fantasy, rather it is a recognition that what is achieved in life is ultimately insubstantial, fleeting and unfulfilling. The term, *sukkha*, the opposite of dukkha, denotes happiness, comfort and ease. The Buddha's insight is only fully understood by looking at the first three noble truths together as a complete analysis of the human situation; but it is already clear from analysing the first Noble Truth that what we wish to achieve lies beyond our reach; not that the goal we seek at any moment is inaccessible, but that the achievement of this goal does not confer the happiness we sought through it. Professional ambition, fame, material wealth, financial security, physical and mental health, romance, admiration and friendship are all understandable goals, but the nature of life is such that we are not fulfilled in our achievements. Whatever we gain in any of these spheres is not enough to satisfy us. Dukkha is a deep-seated internal condition brought about through our relationship with a world which cannot satisfy that which we crave.

However, we cannot fulfill ourselves by changing that world, rather we have to look for a cure for this condition within ourselves. The fundamental reason for this is that the world – in the Buddhist sense of the samsaric realm which we experience – is subject to impermanence. All is impermanent (*anicca*) and subject to change. This is the second aspect of dukkha, in the Buddha's analysis. It is this fact that causes dukkha. We constantly seek to create permanence, to hold on to things, but our aspirations slip through our grasp. This is the important point about the Buddha's description of life being dukkha. Nothing abides: no moment, no feeling, no thought, no person. (This is self-evidently true, at least in the long term, since everybody dies.) However, there are little deaths and new beginnings throughout life – at every moment, in fact. Change is inevitable and necessary; change is the condition of impermanence; impermanence prevents the possibility of anything abiding. This description is neither happy nor sad, optimistic or pessimistic; from a Buddhist viewpoint, it is a true analysis, the analysis of the one who has an enlightened view and sees clearly. However, if we bring any sense of sadness or revulsion to this understanding, then this too is understandable from a Buddhist position, because it points to the next proposition.

The second Noble Truth: the origin of suffering (*Samudaya*)

The second Noble Truth recognises that dukkha goes deeper still, and has even more radical implications.

We are used to thinking about there being *a world I live in* and *I, who live in the world*. In other words, we distinguish quite clearly between ourselves as individuals and the world outside us, which is made up of things, events and people. Whilst this way of understanding ourselves is conventionally and practically useful, it proves dangerous when it becomes rooted too deeply.

Objectively speaking, it would seem highly foolish to suggest that the world – that which is not me – is impermanent, but that *I*, however, *am* permanent. Nevertheless, we often live and think as though that were true. It is as if I am standing alone on a station platform, watching a train go by, and I am aware of the movement of the train; that the people in it are travelling from one place to another; that their lives are changing as they travel along the track between departure and destination; but I am standing still, watching, unmoving, and fully aware of what is happening in front of my eyes.

However, on the train, a person looks out of the window, and as the train passes the station, he sees me standing there alone – in one moment in his present, then just a past image and memory. For me, the passenger moves in time and does not abide; for the passenger I do the same – but the realities perceived are contradictory. In truth, says the Buddha, neither abides. What moves is neither the train nor the person, but the greater, all-embracing, unseen vehicle that passes through train and station alike: time.

Another way of perceiving this view is to imagine standing and staring up at the stars in the night sky, and being aware that what you are seeing is light years away from you and therefore at a considerable distance in *time* from you as well as in *space* (due to the time it takes for their light to reach you). It seems that you are the central fixed point in the universe. Yet now imagine yourself on one of those stars viewing the earth at that same moment. You would not see yourself: you would not yet be there.

Just as Copernicus revolutionised our understanding of the universe, so the Buddha's teaching completely changes the way we understand ourselves. We are also a part of the universe's ceaseless *becoming*; there is no abiding self, but merely a constantly changing and impermanent aspect of that becoming. This Buddhist doctrine of *anatta* (no self) is the third aspect of dukkha; together dukkha, anicca and anatta are known as the three marks, or the fundamental characteristics of being.

This analysis immediately begs the question, 'If there is no self in this sense, what do we consist of? What constitutes an individual?' The

Buddha's answer was that we are a combination of ever-changing forces or energies which can be divided into five groups (aggregates or *skandhas*), which themselves are dukkha. They are dukkha because they cause attachment; in fact, they are the basis of attachment.

The five aggregates

The aggregate of matter

This includes our five material sense organs: eyes, ears, nose, tongue; and 'body and mind' objects: thoughts, ideas and conceptions.

The aggregate of sensations

This includes all sensations: pleasant, unpleasant and neutral. Sensations are experienced through the contact of physical and mental organs with the world and include the creation of visual form, sounds, smells, taste, touch and thoughts or ideas. (Note that, unlike in the Western view, mind is understood to be a sixth sense organ or faculty, because its operation is intrinsic to this activity of contact with, and response to, the world.

The aggregate of perceptions

Perception involves recognition, and arises from sensation in relation to matter. Perceptions are produced through the contact of our six faculties with the external world.

The aggregate of mental formations

By this the Buddha meant volitions, mental acts of will which include intuition, determination, heedlessness and the idea of self. They also include what we previously referred to as the three poisons: desire or craving, ignorance and aversion. The important thing about mental formations is that they are the basis of *karma*, (which we shall return to later), because they are the basis on which we act. The relationship between mental formations and actions is so close that they cannot be separated. As the first two verses of the *Dhammapada* explain:

> What we are today comes from our thoughts of yesterday, and our present thoughts build our life of tomorrow: our life is the

creation of our mind.

If a man speaks or acts with an impure mind, suffering follows him as the wheel of the cart follows the beast that draws the cart.

... If a man speaks or acts with a pure mind, joy follows him as his own shadow.

(Translation: J. Mascaro, Penguin, 1973, p 35)

The aggregate of consciousness

In this context, consciousness does not contain the idea of recognition; rather, it denotes awareness in its most rudimentary form. Consciousness creates awareness of a sense object, so that visual consciousness arises when the eye comes into contact with a colour or form. It is perception that then identifies the colour as blue, or the form as round, for example. The same is true of the process occurring with each of the other sense organs.

The significant issue, from a Buddhist point of view, is that the five aggregates together identify the process of becoming as it takes place in each individual. When we draw this process together into one illustration, its logic is clear in its application to the everyday working of things: I am hungry and I am presented with a plate of food. I *see* it, *smell* it and *anticipate* the taste. I am aware of what is in the dish. *Sensations* arise and *perceptions* follow, with the *recognition* of what it will be like to taste it. *Volition* is brought into play. I wish to eat. I pick up my knife and fork; all other concerns vanish from my mind as I indulge in the pleasure of eating. As my stomach becomes full, my desire decreases. My mind turns to other things. New sensations, perceptions and mental formulations arise. I am more interested in my partner's conversation. I dwell on the discomfort in my stomach. I wish to do other things. I suggest it is time to leave. I look forward to what happens next, or I view it with disappointment – the end of an enjoyable evening and a new working day. I am enveloped in the never-ending process of continual arising (or 'dependent origination'), a chain of cause and effect that never ceases.

A second tangible, but less pleasant, example can be as mundane as having toothache:

> Normally, one simply says 'I have a toothache'. But to Buddhist thinkers this appears as a very inconsistent way of speaking. Neither 'I', nor 'have', nor 'toothache' is counted among the ultimate facts of existence (dharmas). In Buddhist literature, personal

expressions are replaced by impersonal ones. Impersonally, in terms of ultimate events, this experience is divided up into:

1. There is physical form – that is, the tooth as matter.
2. There is a painful feeling.
3. There is sight, touch, and pain-perception (ideation) of the tooth; perception can exist only as ideation.
4. There is, by way of volitional reactions, resentment of pain and desire for physical well-being, etc.
5. There is consciousness, an awareness of all of the above. The 'I' of common-sense talk has thus disappeared; it forms no part of this analysis. It is not the ultimate reality. Not even its components are reality. One might reply, of course, that an imagined 'I' is a part of the actual experience. In that case, it would be listed under consciousness, the last of the five above-mentioned categories. But this consciousness is not ultimate reality. In living human existence there is a continual succession of mental and physical phenomena. It is the union of these phenomena that makes the individual. Every person, or thing, is therefore a putting together, a compound of components which change. In each individual, without any exception, the relationship between its components is always changing, is never the same for two consecutive moments. It follows that no sooner has individuality begun than its dissolution, disintegration, also begins.

(H. Dumoulin and J.C. Maraldo (eds), *Buddhism in the Modern World*, Collier Macmillan, 1979, pp 9–10)

The Buddha's teaching emphasises the fact that life does not have to be like this, moving constantly between desire and aversion; changing states of mind and circumstance within which I identify myself. Desire inevitably leads to aversion, and worldly happiness can never be more than a passing sensation. The only way out of this ceaseless circle is to understand that the 'I' who craves for happiness and contentment is the very obstacle that prevents it. It is born of the ignorance of attachment. Self is dukkha, but letting go of self is true happiness.

The analogy of the chariot

The Buddhist monk Nagasena expressed this understanding in another, more concrete and witty, way, with the analogy of the chariot,

Nagasena is in conversation with King Milinda, who had continually harrassed the local Buddhist monks with his questions and arguments:

'Thereupon the Venerable Nagasena said to King Milinda: 'As a king you have been brought up in great refinement and you avoid roughness of any kind. If you would walk at midday on this hot, burning and sandy ground, then your feet would have to tread on the rough and gritty gravel and pebbles, and they would hurt you; your body would get tired, your mind impaired, and your awareness of your body would be associated with pain. How then did you come – on foot, or on a mount?'

'I did not come, Sir, on foot, but on a chariot.' – 'If you have come on a chariot, then please explain to me what a chariot is. Is the pole the chariot?' – 'No, reverend Sir!' – 'Is then the axle the chariot?' – 'No, reverend Sir!' – 'Is it then the wheels, or the framework, or the flagstaff, or the yoke, or the reins, or the goad-stick?' – 'No, reverend Sir!' – 'Then is it the combination of pole, axle, wheels, framework, flagstaff, yoke, reins and goad which is the "chariot"?' – 'No, reverend Sir!' – 'Then is this "chariot" outside the combination of pole, axle, wheels, framework, flagstaff, yoke, reins and goad?' – 'No, reverend Sir!' – 'Then ask as I may, I can discover no chariot at all. Just a mere sound is this "chariot". But what is the real chariot?'

'Where all constituent parts are present,
The word "a chariot" is applied.
So likewise where the skandhas are,
The term "a being" commonly is used.'

(E. Conze, *Buddhist Scriptures*, Penguin, 1983, pp 148–9)

It is important to be aware that this teaching was not meant to suggest that the absence of selfhood meant annihilation, nor to suggest a consequent lack of meaning or purpose in human life. Were this the case, it would not matter how one behaved, since there would be no person to be blamed. Instinctive desires, whims and wishes could be fulfilled to the full. Hedonism would be the order of the day, for there would be nothing to lose. On the contrary, to see things in this fashion and behave in this way is to bring about the worst of conditions; the way in which this is experienced is through the law of *karma*. Karma also ensures that this sort of analysis of the human situation is not just an academic exercise, a way of cleverly justifying whatever view one finds appealing or conducive to one's own proclivities.

Karmic conditioning

For westerners, the Indian term karma is most often taken to refer to a determinist and fatalist view of human life. Equated with the notion of destiny (but in a pejorative way), it suggests that what happens to an individual is the outcome of unchangeable events, and the best one can do is to suffer the inevitable outcomes in life. This does not accord with the rich interpretation of karma in Indian thought. Karma was a pivotal concept in Indian thinking, around which turned the whole question of why life is as it is. It offered the possibility of different causal explanations for events. The word karma means 'action'. As a result, the relationship between what you do and what happens to you is open to different sorts of explanation. At one end of the scale, it can act as an explanation of why misfortune happens when it is not recognisably the result of particular actions. Common western explanations of this would be 'luck', 'fate' or 'chance'. In other words, where no obvious historical causal connection can be found, the cause must lie elsewhere. In Indian terms, this would relate back to a previous life and its bad karma, which needs to be worked out in this one. Notice, however, the crucial distinction between the western and Indian notions. It is not that what happens is inexplicable or random, but that the explanation lies beyond our everyday cognition or observations. Initial reflection may lead to a form of fatalism ('how can I ever know?'), but this is not necessarily the case.

The reason why karma became a central theme in the Buddha's teaching was because he was concerned with liberating individuals from a state of ignorance and suffering. To see the Buddha's teaching as pessimistic and fatalistic, as some do, is to caricature it in a similar sense as to understand Christianity to be all about sin rather than salvation.

The importance of karma is that is demonstrates the practicality of Buddhist teachings. Ethical considerations become paramount, because liberating oneself from the dis-ease of samsaric existence is a karmic matter, embedded in our everyday activities and behaviour.

Let us take the earlier illustration of reacting to one's desires whilst eating a meal. In this situation, our happiness is always transitory and provisional, because we understand the satisfaction of our desires to be paramount. Such attachment can never remain fulfilling. However, our ignorance prevents us from envisaging any other

way of pursuing life. For a Buddhist, the result of this is more calami-
tous than we might imagine: the effect is cumulative. By not recognising the cumulative effect of our karmic habits, we cannot conceive of
their result. Just like a habit to which we are addicted, so our karmic
conditioning determines our thoughts and deeds. The Buddha saw
this state of being as one of ignorance and craving, over which we
exercise no control. It is strong and blind, and he compared it to thirst
(*tanha*). When we are thirsty, we cannot help desiring water. It
becomes so necessary that we are overwhelmed by it and cannot think
about anything else. Such is the nature of our craving – and yet, in
ignorance, we are oblivious to its effect upon us.

Rebirth

For westerners, even the admission of this unsatisfactoriness would
not equal the importance that the Buddha placed on it. If we only
have one life anyway, we might still affirm the importance of seeking
happiness, through the achievement of our mundane goals. After all
(we might argue), that is all there is; and to have a life of warmth,
food and shelter is infinitely preferable to one in which we lack these
fundamental things.

The Buddha's view rooted karma in the process of rebirth, or
re-becoming. In India this was a generally recognised idea: that we
live through succeeding rebirths which are determined by our karmic
habits. When our actions bring about bad effects, we shall reap their
consequences in a later life. Equally, goods acts will produce a better
rebirth. In this way, the distinction between human and other life
forms is not made. We may be reborn in a higher or lower human situation, and subject to greater or lesser hardship; but we may also be
born in a different form – as an animal, for example, and therefore
subject to even greater ignorance.

In the *Jataka* tales (popular Buddhist fables), the previous
rebirths of the Buddha, as various animals, are recounted: he is reborn
as a bird, a monkey, a buffalo and an elephant amongst others.

It is when the consequences of our ignorance and craving are
recognised in this way, and when the state of affairs is understood as
endless, that the purchase of the Buddha's teaching is registered
more emphatically. The value of a present, relatively comfortable
existence is rendered negligible in the light of future striving.
Imprisoned in *samsara* for life sentence after life sentence, it matters

little whether your present cell offers comparative ease or luxury, since it cannot last.

If we regard karma and rebirth as speculative theories or ideas, it is unlikely that the Buddha's teaching will hit home. We may regard it as a noble and improving guide to living, but not as a salvific message. For Buddhists, rebirth is axiomatic, because it is the teaching of an enlightened mind; a mind which, in the last stages of achieving that enlightened status, actually witnessed its experience of former lives. Western Buddhists often embark on the path without fully accepting this understanding, but the important point is to trust in the Buddha's teaching – even though it may not be fully comprehensible.

One western monk, reticent to undertake ordination, remarked to his teacher that he could not affirm the idea of rebirth. His teacher's reply was that it was not necessary to do so, but that *not* to go for refuge, on the basis that he could not yet affirm it, was tantamount to committing himself to ignorance because he was not already enlightened. It was the practice itself that confirmed the truth or otherwise of the Buddha's teaching. A summary of the Buddhist teaching on samsaric existence, concentrated in the first two noble truths, is depicted in the *Wheel of Becoming*.

The Wheel of Becoming

At the centre of the wheel (its hub) are the three driving forces: ignorance, desire or greed, and aversion, represented by a pig, a cockerel and a snake. These three are linked together, with each biting the others' tail. Surrounding the hub is a circle divided into two, a black and a white half. In the white half the figures are ascending. In the black half they are moving down. This depicts the karmic movement of figures absorbed in rising to a higher state and those, in horror, sinking to a lower existence.

The six realms

The spokes of the wheel separate it into six samsaric realms. At the top are the *devas*, or gods, in their heaven; a place of luxury, pleasure and ease. To their right are the *asuras*, jealous gods, driven by their desire to achieve the top realm and, in so doing, warring with armies. Notice how the tree, rooted in their realm, gives its fruit to the gods above. Their state of mind is epitomised by the figure at the base of

The Tibetan Wheel of Life

the tree seeking to chop it down, in order to achieve the wish fulfilment (symbolised by the fruit). Below them is the animal realm,
where consciousness is duller and ignorance greater. The animals'
constant activity is to find food, by preying on other animals or other
life forms.

In the bottom realm are beings in a tormented state, their consciousness filled with pain and fear as they burn, freeze and undergo
horrific deaths. This is the opposite of the gods' realm: hell as opposed
to heaven.

The next realm upwards is that of the hungry ghosts, or *pretas*.
They are in a state of constant hunger or thirst which can never be
sated. Their enormous, swollen bellies can never be satisfied by the
amount of food they can take in through their thin necks and tiny
mouths. The little fruits of the stunted trees are protected by pro-
truding thorns and sharp branches. Whatever they touch turns to fire
or filth.

The final realm is that of humans. They go about their daily lives,
eating and drinking, giving birth, being treated for sickness, becoming old and frail, being attacked and dying, and carrying on with their
work. Under a tree are two figures, meditating and reflecting on the
sum total of what they see. Here is depicted the suffering that the
Buddha witnessed, and the higher possibility of a precious human
birth to reflect on and escape from it.

These six realms represent the inevitability of past and future
rebirths in different states, since we travel through them and never
abide in any particular realm for ever – not even as gods. They also
represent the states of mind which determine our continual revolu-
tions.

To Buddhists we are part of the ceaseless rhythm of nature, which
flows through us as through everything. In fact to speak of ourselves
is only to speak of this rhythm. The constant motion of every moment
in the rising and falling of the sea; the movement of the river and the
air and our own breathing; thoughts, growth and decay are all one
process at work, becoming and returning in endless cycles. Resisting
this is our attachment to the fiction that we are each abiding entities,
and the frustration this fiction entails is the dukkha that is founded
on a compounded ignorance. Letting go of this, by seeing through
such delusion, is the path to liberation. Beyond this *maya* (the repeated movement of creativity and destruction) lie peace and happiness,
untouched by death and rebirth (which are simply moments of

momentous change in the samsaric cycle, equivalent to the submersion of continents and the arising of new species). The fact that we cannot see what lies beyond is attributable only to our own ignorance and lack of sight or wisdom, which cling to the self as though it were an immutable object. Ignorance is part of that self, its creator in fact. Over time, it can endure no more than a rock in a stream, a leaf in the wind, a pebble on the beach or a cloud in the sky. Our myopic vision, extending from birth to death, is incapable of conceiving this, and so invents the concept of the soul to ensure our eternity. But such an invention merely seals our fate. And far beyond this lies the happiness of the Buddha.

For the gods, pride will eventually cause their downfall. For the asuras, jealousy is their undoing. The animals are conditioned by their instinctive behaviour. The figures in the hell realm cannot escape fear and pain filling their minds. The hungry ghosts are completely absorbed in the need to satisfy their hunger. The humans (although this realm offers the possibility of release), are too absorbed in their own karmic desires and conditioning, their everyday activities, hopes and fears.

We may ourselves identify our own consciousness travelling through these realms at different times, as we experience temporary pleasure and fulfilment, anger and jealousy, instinctive drives, pain and torment (from toothache to heartache), lack of fulfilment and overarching ambition. In the human realm, it is possible to be aware of all these phenomena as they affect us and others, and to observe dispassionately.

In each realm is an encircled Buddha figure, whose teaching is skilfully adapted to those who inhabit it, and is depicted by what he holds in his hands. Everywhere in samsara the truth is available, but it is more accessible to some than to others.

Dependent Origination

The rim of the wheel is divided into twelve segments and scenes. These show how beings pass from one realm to another, and are called the *nidanas*. They are

1 a blind man with a stick
2 a potter with a wheel and pots
3 a monkey climbing a flowering tree
4 a boat with four passengers, one of whom is steering

5 an empty house
6 a man and a woman embracing
7 a man with an arrow in his eye
8 a woman offering a drink to a seated man
9 a man gathering fruit from a tree
10 a pregnant woman
11 a woman giving birth to a child
12 a man carrying a corpse to the cremation ground

These scenes depict Buddhist teaching on *Dependent Origination*: the causal chain which ensures that the Wheel of Samsara keeps revolving. Relating to the figures shown, Dependent Origination states:

1 Because of ignorance, we suffer;
2 Because of ignorance, there arises Will-to-Action;
3 Because of Will-to-Action, Consciousness;
4 Because of Consciousness, Psychophysical Existence;
5 Because of Psychophysical Existence, the Six Organs of Sense (eye, ear, nose, tongue, body [the sense of touch], and mind);
6 Because of the Six Organs of Sense, Contact;
7 Because of Contact, Sensation (or Feeling);
8 Because of Sensation, Craving;
9 Because of Craving, Attachment (or Grasping);
10 Because of Attachment, Becoming (or Worldly Existence);
11 Because of Becoming, Birth;
12 Because of Birth, decay, grief, lamentation, (physical) suffering, dejection, and despair. (All of these constitute suffering in general.)

The Wheel is held by a fearful master with three eyes, fangs and a crown of skulls. He is Yama, the Lord of Death, who has ultimate control over the fate of those who live in samsara, conditioned through their ignorance to see it as reality – as their natural state.

The Wheel can also be understood as a mirror. Yama holds it up to each one of us, and in it we recognise what we understand to be our own reflection – this is what we are. Only through understanding the truth communicated by the Buddha (as when he gave his first *darsana* – teaching – in the Deer Park at Benares, and turned the wheel of the Dharma) can we transform our delusion into knowledge.

The third and fourth Noble Truths explain how this can be done.

The third Noble Truth:
The cessation of suffering (*Nirodha*)

Nirodha means to control. Control of the craving or thirst of attachment is the third teaching. If we accepted only the first two Noble Truths and eschewed the latter two, we would have a teaching about the way things are, but no remedy for this depressing state of affairs. The first two truths diagnose the condition, but the great achievement of the Buddha was to offer a cure; therefore, as far as Buddhists are concerned, he is the physician *par excellence*.

Nirodha is the extinguishing of thirst or craving, to be achieved by rooting out attachment. It results in a state called Nirvana (Nibbana) in which the fires of craving have ceased to burn and there is no more suffering.

One of the problems we have in understanding Nirvana is that this word is used for a state in which something has happened, without describing what that state is actually like. Buddhists maintain that it would be erroneous to speculate about what Nirvana is like, because it would achieve nothing: the important thing is to treat the condition. If we were to ask someone with an apparently incurable disease whether they wished for a newly available cure, they would not stop to speculate about what it would be like once they were cured. If it cured them, they would know they were well, because they would no longer be suffering from their illness. Thus Nirvana may be likened to setting down a heavy load after a long journey, to being released from a worrying debt or being set free from prison. In other words, it is described in terms of a cessation of those things which cause suffering.

As with all illness, of course, the proposed cure is of no value unless you accept the diagnosis, so this third truth is to be understood in the light of the first two. The possibility of Nirvana cannot be realised unless our present existence is understood as dukkha.

Buddhist scriptures use many metaphors to contrast dukkha and Nirvana. One of the starkest is that used in the *Fire Sermon*:

The Fire Sermon
Bhikkhus, all is burning. And what is the all that is burning? Bhikkhus, the eye is burning, visible forms are burning, visual consciousness is burning, visual impression is burning, also

whatever sensation, pleasant or painful or neither-pleasant-nor-painful, arises on account of the visual impression, that too is burning. Burning with what? Burning with the fire of lust, with the fire of hate, with the fire of delusion; I say it is burning with birth, ageing and death, with sorrows, with lamentations, with pains, with grief, with despairs.

(W. Rahula, *What The Buddha Taught*, Gordon Fraser, 1982, p 95)

The Buddha recounts the same experience for all the senses, the body and the mind; he explains that one who knows this becomes dispassionate, and,

Being dispassionate, he becomes detached, through detachment he is liberated. When liberated there is knowledge that he is liberated. And he knows: Birth is exhausted, the holy life has been lived, what has to be done is done, there is no more left to be done on this account.

(W. Rahula, *What The Buddha Taught*, Gordon Fraser, 1982, pp 96–7)

Nirvana

In another darsana he speaks of Nirvana as 'getting rid of all cares and troubles' (*Sabbasava sutta*). Other poetic terms which he uses include: the harbour of refuge; the cool cave; the home of ease; the place of bliss.

Perhaps the greatest difficulty for non-Buddhists is that we want to understand Nirvana through ideas and language with which we are already familiar. Thus, we might equate 'Nirvana' with 'heaven', and expect to find luxuriant and elaborate descriptions of how life there will be immeasurably better than in the here and now. This conception is fraught with problems, because Nirvana is part of a world view constructed in quite a different way. There is a continuing selfhood in heaven which Nirvana denies; there is a tendency to understand heaven as a future state, following on from earthly life, that Nirvana is not; there is a belief that heaven is, at least to some degree, understandable in earthly terms, whereas Nirvana is not even the opposite of samsaric existence. Samsaric existence entails the cessation of everything.

The problem we then have is that Nirvana sounds dreadfully negative, as though everything precious to us is denied and destroyed. The Buddhist response to this is that speculation of this kind is simply unhelpful. Nirvana is realised in the midst of our everyday existence:

He who has realised the Truth, Nirvana, is the happiest being in the world. He is free from all 'complexes' and obsessions, the worries and troubles that torment others. His mental health is perfect. He does not repent the past, nor does he brood over the future. He lives fully in the present. Therefore he appreciates and enjoys things in the purest sense without self-projections. He is joyful, exultant, enjoying the pure life, his faculties pleased, free from anxiety, serene and peaceful. As he is free from selfish desire, hatred, ignorance, conceit, pride and all such 'defilements', he is pure and gentle, full of universal love, compassion, kindness, sympathy, understanding and tolerance. His service to others is of the purest, for he has no thought of self. He gains nothing, accumulates nothing, not even anything spiritual, because he is free from the illusion of Self, and the 'thirst' for becoming.

(W. Rahula, *What the Buddha Taught*, Gordon Fraser, 1982, p 43)

So, rather than speculate, we must discern this way of being in the examples of others and cultivate it in ourselves. The Buddhist teacher, Nagasena, was once asked:

'Venerable Nagasena, does he who has not received Nirvana know how happy a state Nirvana is?'
'Yes, he knows it.'
'But how can he know that without his receiving Nirvana?'
'Now what do you think. . ? Do those whose hands and feet have not been cut off know how sad a thing it is to have them cut off?'
'Yes, Sir, that they know!'
'But how do they know it?'
'Well, by hearing the sound of the lamentation of those whose hands and feet have been cut off, they know it.'
'Just so . . . it is by hearing the glad words of those who have seen Nirvana that they who have not received it know how happy a state it is.'

(E. Conze, *Buddhist Scriptures*, Penguin, 1983, p 156)

Here we are confronted with an apparent paradox in Buddhist thinking. If our aim is to cultivate peace, ease, bliss and well-being in ourselves, does this not make Nirvana or enlightenment a selfish goal? How can it equate with the Buddha's emphasis on the extinction of self (*anatta*)? The Buddhist answers that this is a misunderstanding of why these goals are sought. The self is composed of self-centredness, which arises from attachment or craving. It constantly needs to be re-affirmed – and yet such re-affirmation is ultimately unattainable, because this self is a fiction. Throughout our everyday lives we look for this affirmation from those around us. When someone praises me I feel confident and happy. When I am blamed or deprecated I feel anxious, even angry. When someone else is praised I feel jealous; I experience envy. These negative states of mind are a result of attachment to my own self-centredness; even my positive states of mind depend on the same thing. In this condition I cannot freely give and be altruistic. When we speak of cultivating Nirvana it is not dependent on my self-centredness, my ego, being affirmed. It is a release from that need. In this release it is possible to give without receiving, to offer loving kindness without first being its recipient. Freed from this flux of emotions and mental instability, I can now act freely and give when needed. I am also able to direct my attention to others' needs, rather than being preoccupied by my own. An enlightened state of mind is one in which this creative giving occurs spontaneously and without hindrance. Were the qualities inherent in an enlightened mind to be cultivated for the ego's own sake, i.e. if that were the motivation, then they could not be achieved.

In Camus' novel *The Fall*, we encounter a character who sees through such self-deceit, and opts out from the status and respect he is accorded because of his mistrust of his own motives. Similarly, from a Buddhist point of view, the self-delusion this character formerly suffered from could not result in the ease, equanimity and contentment that is conferred by the extinguishing of craving. For this reason, the path to Nirvana involves overcoming specific obstacles in oneself. This is expressed in the *Five Hindrances* (*Nivarana*): attachment to sensuality; ill-will; torpor of mind or body; worry; and wavering doubt. Reflecting on these purifies understanding and counteracts such self-deceit. By reflecting on and learning from them a greater awareness occurs. One teacher puts it as follows:

> All these feelings of hunger or thirst or restlessness or jealousy or fear, of lust and greed and sleepiness – all these we can regard as teachers. Rather than resenting them, saying: 'What did I do to deserve this?' you should say: 'Thank you very much. I'll have to learn this lesson some day, I might as well do it now, rather than put it off.'

(Ven. Ajahn Sumedho, *Cittaviveka: Teachings from the Silent Mind*,
Amaravati Publications, 1992, p 68)

The fourth Noble Truth: The path to the cessation of suffering (*Magga*)

This is known as the 'Middle Way', and avoids the two extremes of indulgence in sensual pleasures and self-mortification. It is also known as the 'Noble Eightfold Path', because it outlines eight categories through which purity of mind, calm and insight can be achieved.

These eight divisions are grouped into three aspects of Buddhist practice: Ethical Conduct (*Sila*); Mental Discipline (*Samadhi*); Wisdom (*Panna* or *Prajna*).

The Eightfold Path

1 Right Understanding (*Samma ditthi*)
2 Right Intention or Orientation
   (*Samma sankappa*)   **Wisdom**
3 Right Speech (*Samma vaca*)
4 Right Action (*Samma kammanta*)   **Ethical Conduct**
5 Right Livelihood (*Samma ajiva*)
6 Right Effort (*Samma vayama*)
7 Right Mindfulness (*Samma sati*)   **Mental Discipline**
8 Right Concentration (*Samma samadhi*)

As with all things in Buddhism, it is important to understand the interrelationships of these categories. The Eightfold Path is sometimes likened to a ladder with eight rungs, as though one might develop by practising each discipline in turn. This is a misleading idea, because the Buddha stressed that progress is made by the practice of each aspect of the path in concert with the others.

For example, it is important to recognise that Ethical Conduct is absolutely necessary in order to achieve Wisdom, and that without Mental Discipline we lack the capacity for Ethical Conduct. Similarly, therefore, the achievement of Compassion and Wisdom, which are the characteristics of an Enlightened One, cannot be gained separately and are not distinct. Everything goes hand in hand. The wise person is the one who acts compassionately, the compassionate person is the one who acts wisely.

One who treads the Eightfold Path is, therefore, doing something quite different from one who 'wanders' on the Wheel of Becoming. He or she recognises the possibility of improvement and eventual emancipation and, acting on that possibility – with the Buddha's teaching and his or her own practice as the guide, alongside others who are treading the path – works creatively toward a more refined awareness of how to live well. The Eightfold Path is like a map which charts this journey; its practice is like the raft to the other shore.

Ethical Conduct

The Buddha said his teachings were 'for the good of the many, for the happiness of the many, out of compassion for the world'. If Ethical Conduct does not arise through following the teachings, then they are of no use whatsoever. The quality of compassion is the pinnacle of Buddhist achievement, and Ethical Conduct therefore is not an end in itself but a means to develop compassion. It is the cultivation of loving kindness, generosity and forgiveness. These qualities will manifest themselves in our activity in the world, in that which we give out in Right Speech, Right Action and Right Livelihood. To the extent that these are practised, so we will decrease the suffering of others and ourselves. We shall also purify ourselves. Understanding and practising these three aspects of the path should not be seen simply as a matter of duty and discipline. Certainly it is that, but it is more. Ultimately, such actions should become effortless and spontaneous, rather than a matter of grim resolution.

Right Speech means abstaining from telling lies, slandering and promoting division and emnity, using abusive language, and indulging in careless gossip. In some cases, if one cannot say something helpful, it is better to keep a noble silence.

Right Action promotes peaceful and harmonious conduct. It has exactly the same aims as right speech, but a different form of expression. Doing that which causes harm to others is its exact opposite, whether this be through taking life, stealing or taking advantage of someone sexually.

Right Livelihood determines that one should abstain from making a living through causing harm, whether by trading in arms or intoxicating drinks, killing animals or cheating.

All these abstentions are indications of what does not improve the lives of others or ourselves; but we need to analyse the reasons why this is so important. On one level it is clear that the quality of life is dependent on our conduct. When someone does an injustice to me, in word or deed, I immediately feel aggrieved. Anger arises, and I want to hit back in some way. My state of mind is imbalanced, and I am tempted to act hastily and without due thought for the consequences. Multiply this by the number of acts of this kind committed, and we move from individual antagonism to social unrest – and ultimately to war. Look around the world and you will see that the effect of this is endemic. It is not that this happens sporadically, but that there is a perpetual chain of events caused by the continual cycle of such activities. They have a momentum evoked through the mind and hearts of individuals and groups which engulfs us at work, in the home and even between friends. This momentum has a history in individual lives and within nations that is hard to rectify. Its result is a lack of trust and willingness to put things right. For Buddhists, this is part and parcel of karmic conditioning; the law of cause and effect that ensures samsaric existence continues to flourish. The only way to reverse this process is to take responsibility for it individually, and determine not to contribute to it. Unless individuals alone decide that in the context of their own lives and sphere of influence they are going to behave differently, there can be no diminishing of this state of affairs. This is dukkha in action, and there is no other agency to which we can appeal for help but ourselves. *Sila* is the only antidote to dukkha; there is no other palliative and no other way of aspiring to true happiness. However, the point about Sila being an aspect of the Eightfold Path is that Ethical Conduct is not attainable without Mental Discipline and Wisdom.

Mental Discipline

The Buddha addressed his brethren thus: 'It is through not understanding and not grasping the Four Noble Truths, O brethren, that we have had to run for so long, to wander for so long in this weary path of transmigration, both you and I.'

The power of the Noble Truths lies in this aspect of mental discipline: Right Effort, Right Mindfulness and Right Concentration. Without these nothing is attainable. Right Effort involves preventing evil and unwholesome states of mind from arising; ridding oneself of such unwholesome states of mind that have already arisen; producing, or causing to arise, good and wholesome states of mind and bringing them to perfection. This necessitates generating the will for this to happen, and a single-minded application to the task. Without effort, which is itself an act of will, doubt, anxiety and other hindrances will distract the mind from its task. We are reminded here of numerous crucial events in the Buddha's life which could have been resolved quite differently: the episode of going forth and leaving his loved ones; the exertion of denying Mara's temptations; ignoring Brahma's exhortations to preach the dharma. Without Right Effort and its motivation of the will, it is difficult not to be sidetracked into admitting the possibility of a different way of dealing with things, and of thinking of one's goal as being over-ambitious, idealistic or extreme.

Right Mindfulness provides the context for Right Effort. It relates it to the here and now. It is concerned with immediate states of consciousness, not speculative possibilities. It involves diligent awareness of the activities of the body, sensations and feelings; the activities of the mind, and ideas, thoughts and conceptions. In other words, it monitors what is actually going on. Without mindfulness effort would be blind, random and ineffectual. Without effort mindfulness would be barren and unproductive. Without both, morality, or ethical conduct, would be no more than just a duty.

Right Concentration underpins Right Mindfulness. Without concentration mindfulness, let alone Ethical Conduct, is impossible. Concentration is a fundamental skill, in that is develops attentiveness. In the various schools of Buddhism it is practised in different ways, but all concentrate on attention to detail, bringing the capacity of the mind to a full awareness of every thought, action and sensation. One of the basic practices is concentration on breathing (*anapanasati*). If Right Mindfulness is a matter of awareness, Right Concentration is the basis upon which that awareness is attained. Being able to be aware of the process of breathing – a fundamental physiological function – enables us to discern what is actually happening. When this concentration is applied to sensations and feelings; the activities of the mind; the ideas, thoughts and conceptions that arise and fall away in our mental habits; then a true understanding of the way things are, is arrived at. It is all too easy to rationalise what is going on in ourselves as individuals, such that we affirm our desires and longings, but the antidote to this is to present ourselves with evidence for things being otherwise. The purpose of Right Concentration is to attain a focus of mind that cannot be knocked off balance by inclinations that arise as a result of desire or craving. For example, in an attitude of meditation, or within our daily life, we may suffer from boredom and seek to relieve it by pursuing a different goal that will produce immediate pleasure or interest. Immediately, our efforts are put into achieving this aim. We are no longer mindful of the overall context in which we live, nor the wish to follow the dharma, and we pursue short-term pleasure and happiness. Our concentration is then not connected to what is happening in our bodies and minds, but to how we might achieve what we momentarily crave. We are no longer in control of what is going on, we simply serve the interests of that desire which has arisen.

Right Effort, Right Mindfulness and Right Concentration are the safeguards against such forgetfulness and the foundation of Sila.

Wisdom

Wisdom consists in Right Intention or Orientation and Right Understanding. They are dependent on Right Mindfulness, since Right Thought constitutes selfless renunciation or detachment (as opposed to *attachment*, outlined previously) and Right Understanding is the realisation of things as they are (as opposed to suffering the delusion that arises from pursuing desires).

Wisdom is not the result of cleverness or intellectual capacity, which are as much prey to karmic inclinations as any other capacity of mind. This is a common misreading of the Buddha's teaching, since it is presumed that following the logic of such an analytical summary of human experience necessitates great intellectual acumen. But cleverness can be as much an obstacle as it can be an aid to wisdom. It can be a tool used to proliferate self-deceit, as well as being used to cut through it. Wisdom is the summation of what has already been practised, but Right Intention or Orientation and Right Understanding are also the basis of the practice itself, since they are the motivation for Right Effort and the further aspects of the path. Clearly, therefore, wisdom can be seen as the final factor of enlightenment, but it is also cumulative; a refinement that grows as thought and understanding become progressively freed from ignorance. This unfettering is gained by practising the path as a whole. The term that sums up this process is 'bhavana', or mental development. It involves a devotional aspect, in that it is a wholehearted commitment to self-transformation. It also has a reflective aspect, in that it demands an awareness of what is happening in the here and now. It involves a highly practical aspect, in that it has a necessary purchase on the way we act in every situation. Different Buddhist movements address these forms of practice in their own particular ways, but all concur on the need to address all three.

The result of this path, pursued to its conclusion, has been preserved in the words of the Buddha, addressing his disciple Ananda, concerning the question of the mystery of death, when close to his own eventual passing:

> Those who have died after the complete destruction of the three bonds of lust, of covetousness, and of the egotistical cleaving to existence, need not fear the state after death. They will not be in a state of suffering; their minds will not continue as a Karma of evil deeds or sin, but are assured of final deliverance. When they die, nothing will remain of them but their good thoughts, their righteous acts, and the bliss that proceeds from truth and righteousness. As rivers must at last reach the distant main, so their minds will be reborn in higher states of existence and continue to press on to their ultimate goal, which is the ocean of truth, the eternal peace of Nirvana.
>
> Men are anxious about death and their fate after death; but there is nothing strange in this, that a human being must die. However, that you should inquire about them, and having heard the truth still be anxious about the dead, this is wearisome to the Blessed One . . . .
>
> Hell is destroyed for me, and rebirth as an animal, or a spirit, or in any place of woe. I am converted; I am no longer liable to be reborn in a state of suffering, and am assured of final deliverance.
>
> (H. Dumoulin and J.C. Maraldo (eds), *Buddhism in the Modern World*, Collier Macmillan, 1976, p 21)

4
BUDDHIST
—— SCRIPTURES ——
AND SCHOOLS

Like other religious traditions, Buddhism has divided into various branches over its history, and its scriptures reflect this diversity.

After teaching for forty-five years, the Buddha died at the age of eighty. This is called his *paranirvana*, and is seen as a final release from the round of rebirth. His teachings were memorised by his followers and passed on by oral tradition. By 480 BCE a council was called to ratify the Buddha's teachings. The aim of this council, held in Rajgir, was to agree a definitive version of the Buddha's message.

By 380 BCE, a second council was called at Vesali to ensure that the *Vinaya* – the code of discipline – was adhered to by all Buddhist monks. At this gathering, differences of opinion arose as to what the Buddha actually taught. At this point the first division in the Buddha's followers arose. This division increased until, eventually, two main schools in Buddhism emerged. One became known as the *Mahayana*, meaning Great Vehicle, and the other comprised a number of more conservative groups, of which the surviving example was the *Theravada*, meaning 'way of the elders'. The Mahayana spread north-west from India into present-day Nepal, China, Tibet, Japan, Korea and Vietnam. Theravada Buddhism spread southwards into Sri Lanka, Burma, Thailand, Cambodia and Laos.

Palm leaf with Buddha image

—— **The Theravada Scriptures** ——

It is said that the first Buddhist scriptures were written down by Theravada monks at the fourth council in Sri Lanka, during the 1st century BCE. They used the ancient colloquial Indian language of Pali, spoken by the Buddha. The scriptures were written on palm leaves and became known as the *Pali canon* or *Tipitaka*. The term Tipitaka means 'three baskets', which refers to the threefold division of the scriptures, known as *Vinaya Pitaka*, *Sutta Pitaka* and *Abhidhamma Pitaka*.

The *Tipitaka*

The *Vinaya* is the book of discipline for monks containing the 227 rules by which they must live. The *Sutta Pitaka* contains the teachings of the Buddha on the Four Noble Truths, Eightfold Path and the popular Buddhist literature that constitutes the *Dhammapada* and the *Jataka Tales*. *Sutta* means 'thread', and indicates the connection seen to exist between the different teachings of the Buddha that constitutes the overall world view of the tradition. *Dhammapada* means 'path of Truth'. It consists of an anthology of the Buddha's sayings, collected between 563 and 483 BCE. They act as a source of guidance for Buddhists everywhere but especially for those in the Theravada tradition. The *Jataka Tales* are a collection of stories of the Buddha's previous lives. They focus on the Ten Perfections which lead to perfect Buddhahood: generosity, virtue, renunciation, wisdom, energy, patience, truthfulness, resolution, loving kindness and an even temper. The *Abhidhamma Pitaka* contains the more philosophical teachings which underpin the Buddhist understanding of life. They were intended as a basis of the Buddhist outlook which opposed other Indian conceptions of reality. They are essentially philosophical and psychological, arguing the Buddhist perspective against other prevailing philosophical positions in the Indian sub-continent, and are the source of its doctrinal formulations.

The *Dhammapada*

The *Dhammapada*, however, remains the most common source of inspiration to which lay Buddhists refer. Its teachings and value can perhaps best be indicated by quoting from the text itself.
The verses below refer to controlling the mind:

> The mind is wavering and restless, difficult to guard and restrain: let the wise man straighten his mind as a maker of arrows makes his arrows straight . . . .
> The mind is fickle and flighty, it flies after fancies wherever it likes: it is difficult indeed to restrain. But it is a great good to control the mind; a mind self-controlled is a source of great joy . . . .
> An enemy can hurt an enemy, and a man who hates can hurt another man; but a man's own mind, if wrongly directed, can do him a far greater harm.
> A father or a mother, or a relative, can indeed do good to a man; but his own right-directed mind can do to him a far greater good.
> (*Dhammapada*, trans J. Mascaro, Penguin, 1973, p 40)

The *Jatakas*

Equally, the example of the Buddha on his route to enlightenment through previous lives, is exemplified in the following story from the *Jatakas*:

The Bodhisattva and the Hungry Tigress

The Buddha told the following story to Ananda: Once upon a time, in the remote past, there lived a king, Maharatha by name. He was rich in gold, grain and chariots, and his power, strength, and courage were irresistible. He had three sons who were like young gods to look at. They were named Mahapranada, Mahadeva and Mahasattva.

One day the king went for relaxation into a park. The princes delighted with the beauties of the park and the flowers which could be seen everywhere, walked about here and there until they came to a large thicket of bamboos. There they dismissed their servants, in order to rest for a while. But Mahapranada said to his two brothers: 'I feel rather afraid here. There might easily be some wild beasts about, and they might do us harm.' Mahadeva replied: 'I also feel ill at ease. Though it is not my body I fear for. It is the thought of separation from those I love which terrifies me.'

As the princes strolled about in the solitary thicket they saw a tigress, surrounded by five cubs, seven days old. Hunger and thirst had exhausted the tigress, and her body was quite weak. On seeing her, Mahapranada called out: 'The poor animal suffers from having given birth to the seven cubs only a week ago! If she finds nothing to eat, she will either eat her own young or die from hunger!' Mahasattva replied: 'How can this poor exhausted creature find food?' Mahapranada said: 'Tigers live on fresh meat and warm blood.' Mahadeva said: 'She is quite exhausted, overcome by hunger and thirst, scarcely alive and very weak. In this state she cannot possibly catch any prey. And who would sacrifice himself to preserve her life?' Mahapranada said: 'Yes, self-sacrifice is so difficult!'

Greatly agitated, the three brothers carefully watched the tigress for some time, and then went towards her. But Mahasattva thought to himself: 'Now the time has come for me to sacrifice myself! For a long time I have served this putrid body and given it beds and clothes, food and drink, and conveyances of all kinds. Yet it is doomed to perish and fall down, and in the end it will break up and be destroyed. How much better to leave this ungrateful body of one's own accord in good time! It cannot subsist for ever, because it is like urine which must come out.

Today I will use it for a sublime deed.

For the weal of the world I wish to win enlightenment, incomparably wonderful. From deep compassion I now give away my body, so hard to quit, unshaken in my mind.'

The friendly prince then threw himself down in front of the tigress. But she did nothing to him. The Bodhisattva noticed that she was too weak to move. As a merciful man he had taken no sword with him. He therefore cut his throat with a sharp piece of bamboo, and fell down near the tigress. She noticed the Bodhisattva's body all covered with blood, and in no time ate up all the flesh and blood, leaving only the bones.

'It was I, Ananda, who at that time and on that occasion was that prince Mahasattva.'

(E. Conze (trans), *Buddhist Scriptures*, Penguin Classics, 1959, pp 24–26)

The significance of this story is, of course, not that we should look for opportunities to sacrifice ourselves, but that we should recognise the need to act compassionately. Not an easy task in the course of life, but a signal that our own value lies beyond our usual preoccupations.

The Arahant

The highest aspiration in Theravada Buddhism is to become an *Arahant* (*Arhat*), or one who has passed beyond the fetters of samsaric existence.

> Ah happy indeed the Arahants! In them is no craving found. The 'I am' conceit is rooted out; confusion's net is burst, lust free they have attained; translucent is the mind of them.
>
> (*Samyutta – nikaya* lll, 83)

The Arahant is the ideal of the Theravadin school. The word refers to those saints or sages who, having followed the Buddha's teachings, upon death, will enter into Nibbana (Nirvana). They are fully emancipated.

The scriptures describe an arahant by a standard formula, as one in whom the 'outflows' (sense desire, becoming, ignorance, wrong views) have 'dried up'; one who has 'done what has to be done'. However, the question remained (and later exercised Buddhist thinkers) as to the distinction between an Arahant and a Buddha. It was this distinction that the Mahayana school exploited, indicating that the ideal of arahantship and the goal of Nibbana were inferior to the larger aspiration of Buddhahood and the Bodhisattva path (described later), which accentuated the virtues of compassion, and of gaining emancipation for the sake of others rather than for one's own entry into Nirvana.

Other examples of teachings from the Theravada Scriptures have been quoted in the previous chapters. The following sections will therefore illustrate the scriptures of the different Mahayana schools.

——— The Mahayana Scriptures ———

The spread of Buddhism in different directions resulted in a diversity of doctrines and scriptures. For the Theravadins, the authenticity of the scriptures was determined by which texts, historically, actually came from the Buddha himself. But in opposition to this, Mahayana Buddhists asserted that certain other scriptures were just as authoritative, even though they could not be traced back to the Buddha in a historical way. They claimed authority more by mythological connection than historical. For example, the *Prajna Paramita Sutras* (the teachings on Perfect Wisdom), which are scriptures of great significance in the Mahayana tradition, are said to have been revealed by the Buddha himself, but were too difficult to be understood by his contemporaries. Because of this they were stored in the palace of the *Nagas* (serpents) in the Nether World. When the time was right to reveal them the great Buddhist thinker, Nagarjuna, brought them back into the human realm.

The Mahayana scriptures are written in the ancient, classical Indian language of Sanskrit. Mahayana texts vary in form and introduce both mythological and philosophical features not found in the *Theravada*. Siddhartha, the historical Buddha, often takes on a more mystical and poetic character. An important development reveals that he was not the only Buddha: there were others before him and others yet to come. Visiting a Tibetan shrine room, one is struck by the plethora of forms of enlightened beings. These represent particular qualities or energies, and appear not in strictly naturalistic form, but expressing their symbolic significance. Thus, for example, Avalokiteshvara represents the quality of compassion, Manjushri represents the quality of wisdom.

Avalokiteshvara

Manjushri

Most significantly, in one of these representations Avalokiteshvara has one thousand hands, each containing an eye. This indicates his ability to see all and extend his service to the suffering of all living beings. Manjushri wields a sword which represents the capacity of wisdom to cut through all ignorance.

Behind these representations is the development of doctrine, which serves to explain them.

The Bodhisattva

The *Bodhisattva*, literally *bodhi* (enlightened) and *sattva* (essence), is a being who delays his entry into Nirvana in order to help all sentient beings. Out of compassion, he or she returns to the samsaric realm to help others along the path.

The *Diamond Sutra* says: 'A bodhisattva is not attached to anything when he gives, like a person in the daylight who can see things as they really are.' For this reason Mahayana Buddhists take what is called the Bodhisattva vow, which states:

> The deluding passions are inexhaustible.
> I vow to extinguish them all.
> Sentient beings are numberless.
> I vow to save them all.
> The truth is impossible to expound.
> I vow to expound it.
> The way of the Buddha is unattainable.
> I vow to attain it.

Such an exercise in idealism has to have a rationale. This is located in the Mahayana emphasis on no-self, which denies individualism or 'self-ness' in all its forms. The *Diamond Sutra* explains this in the following way:

> If a Bodhisattva has any notion of a being, a person, or a self, he could not be called a bodhisattva. A bodhisattva should not give a gift while basing himself on the notion of form, sound, smell, taste, touch, or while basing himself on any thought. He should give without the notion of a giver or a gift. That great being who gives without basing himself on any notion, his merit is not easy to measure.
>
> (*Diamond Sutra 3*)

This idea is based on the teachings of the *Prajna Paramita*. The wisdom of a Bodhisattva is perfect, and goes beyond the wisdom of the world. It fully understands the absence of abiding entities, such as selfhood. It is based on the notion of *sunyata*, meaning emptiness or void. So the *Heart Sutra* states:

> In emptiness there is no form, nor feeling, nor perception, nor impulse, nor consciousness; no eye, ear, nose, tongue, body, mind; no forms, sounds, smells, tastes, touchables or objects of mind; no sight-organ elements, and so forth until we come to no mind-consciousness element.
>
> (*Heart Sutra 5*)

Here we have arrived at a highly abstruse philosophical position which, nevertheless, has important practical consequences. In order to live well in this world, attain our inherent Buddha-nature, and avoid rebirth, selflessness has to be realised through developing wisdom and compassion. So, in the *Mahayana*, cultivating insight and devotion go hand in hand. This creative process neither ignores the intellect nor renders it supreme. As a consequence, the relationship between the monastic Sangha and lay life becomes closer. The way to Buddhahood becomes broader, without lessening the qualities aspired to. The Bodhisattva path is rooted in the practice of the six perfections: patience, giving, morality, vigour, meditation and wisdom. The difficulties encountered in this are poetically described in the career of Avalokiteshvara.

Avalokiteshvara

It is said that Avalokiteshvara was entrusted with the task of rescuing all living beings from samsara. In attempting to accomplish this he grew exhausted and despaired. At this moment he gave vent to tears that fell to the ground and grew as lotuses (illustrating the creative power of his compassion). From these lotus flowers were born the Bodhisattvas Green and White Tara. Their destiny was to assist him in his task. As an indication of this, Green Tara is always depicted with one foot released from the meditation posture towards the ground, illustrating her readiness to come to the aid of suffering beings. There is also a story that removes Tara from the mythological realm, indicating not only the practicality of the doctrine of compassion, but also the ignorance of thinking that form is the means of detecting the presence of a compassionate being. This story goes as follows:

> In lifetime after lifetime Tara has manifested in female form, demonstrating that enlightenment is attainable by all – men and women alike.
>
> Once there was a lone traveller making his perilous way across the forbidding plateau of Tibet. Exhausted and without food he was in immediate danger of losing his life when he came across a young girl tending a herd of yaks. She took the weary man into her tent, nursed him back to health and fed him until his strength returned. As the man was recovering he observed that the young girl was alone. Single-handedly she was doing the work that even a number of strong men would have found difficult. Eventually he was fit to travel again and the girl sent him on his way with a bag of provisions. Although it was a long journey, the man discovered that the food she had given him never ran out until he was back in his own valley again. Marvelling at all that had happened he thought, 'Perhaps that girl was actually Tara!' When he went to his lama and told him the story, the

lama upbraided him saying 'Of course she was Tara, you block-head! How stupid of you not to recognise her. You must have a strong connection with her, but if you ever want to see her again you had better purify your delusions and practise harder.'

(J. Landaw, *Tara's Colouring Book*, Wisdom Publications, 1979)

Green Tara and White Tara

The Three Body Doctrine

Clearly, this development of the idea of Buddhahood to include the historical Buddha, Buddhas of other ages, and the principle of sunya-ta, or voidness, needed to be systematically expounded; we find this in the Three Body (Trikaya) Doctrine.

The historical Buddha (Siddhartha Gautama) was identified as the *Nirmanakaya* (form body), a particular expression in one place and time of the eternal truths of the Dharma. The *Dharmakaya* was identified as the eternal principle of Truth, which transcended space and time. Through meditation and devotion Buddhists came to describe images of Buddhas which are not historical but which are archetypal. These are identified as *Sambhogakaya* (bliss bodies). Each of these different images represents a particular aspect of the enlightenment experience. They are a more refined understanding of the nature of enlightenment than the Buddha as an historical figure, pointing to the more abstract awareness of the idea of the ultimate truth expressed in the idea of Dharmakaya.

The Lotus Sutra

The *Lotus Sutra*, or *Lotus of the True Law (Saddharma Pundarika)* is often referred to by some Mahayana Buddhists as the final teaching of the Buddha, and thus has a venerated place in the *Mahayana Canon*. One emphasis for which it is acclaimed is its teaching on 'upaya' or 'skill in means'. We have already referred to skilfulness but it is expounded at great length in this particular text.

The *Lotus Sutra* explains that there are different teachings used by the Buddha to encourage the faithful to perfect Buddhahood, according to their individual propensities and capacities. All the same, though there may be said to be many paths to the same goal, they all constitute aspects of one vehicle, that is, one overall path, that of the Bodhisattva Mahasattva or Great Being. However, the *Lotus Sutra* allows the Buddhist message to become available to all, relative to their particular capacities. It is an acknowledgement that people do not start in the same place with regard to their apprehension of the truth. In much the same way, to teach quantum physics to a child would be an unproductive way of furthering their development. This idea is explained in the *Parable of the Burning House*. Again, we see the emphasis on the practical significance of teaching in Buddhism. The *Lotus Sutra* acknowledges that it is not one's

---

The Parable of the Burning House

A father owns an old house which, while he is out, catches on fire. He hears his own children still playing in the house, unaware that it is burning. Absorbed in their amusement, the children pay no attention to their father calling them out of the house. He then tells them he has special carts of different kinds for each of them to play with, and encourages the children to run out and find them. Once out of the house and free from danger, they find the carts are all the same – but better than any of them had expected.

The burning house is the samsaric world in which, foolishly, we are absorbed, like the children. The father is the Buddha who finds a way to deliver us from our predicament through his skill

---

in means (upaya). Firstly, he offers gifts to get the children out of the house. Secondly, he offers them their *favourite* carts to encourage each of them.

From the perspective of the *Lotus Sutra*, the inferior carts represent the early teachings of the *Hinayana* (lesser vehicle) which, nevertheless, were a skilful means of getting the Buddha's followers to start on the path that leads to Nirvana. The final, best cart that the children find outside the house represents the higher ideal of perfect Buddhahood, as taught in this sutra.

understanding at the beginning of the journey that matters, but whether the teacher can skilfully lead his or her pupils to the appropriate final understanding. Thus this teaching recognises that the Dharma is understood by various means and achieved by different strategies. It constitutes a pragmatic realism that is nevertheless not open-ended, but carefully planned. It allows for a great diversity in the same way that the branches of Mahayana Buddhism developed without causing schism. This served the tradition well as it transplanted itself into the various cultures of China, Tibet and Japan.

The *Lotus Sutra* is not an easy text to read. It does not have the strict formulation of the Theravada Scriptures. Rather, it reads like a mystery play set in a super-mundane world, where the Lord Buddha reveals the immense span of his existences and the illusory way in which he appears to enter Nirvana, but actually continues his Bodhisattva career endlessly for the salvation of all beings. He appears in whatever guise is suitable for the furtherance of his subjects, and offers them teachings and practices suitable to their capacities. Gone is the austerity of Theravada practice as a single route to Nirvana. The world is a phantasmagorical place quite beyond the ken of ordinary mortals.

Emphasis on faith in the Buddha's authority to release us from suffering is a key theme. The Buddha states:

> I reveal the law in its multifariousness with regard to the inclinations and dispositions of creatures.
>
> I use different means to raise each according to his own character. Such is the might of my knowledge.
>
> (*Lotus Sutra 2*)

and

> Hence we will raise many Bodhisattvas by the display of skilfulness and the encouraging of the wish of obtaining fruits.
>
> (Lotus Sutra 2)

In his omniscience the Buddha reveals that the destiny of all creatures is Buddhahood – nothing less. The most important issue is erasing the self-imposed ignorance that blinds beings from seeing the truth. Even devout Buddhists suffer this continuing blindness. A constant theme of the *Sutra* is that Theravada Buddhists are blinded by their short-sighted conception of Nirvana as the ultimate goal. Arhathood (the saintly aim of the Theravadins) and Pratyekabuddhahood (the aim of those who have become enlightened, but who have chosen not to preach the Dharma to others) are indications of this limited awareness. What has now been revealed is far beyond their thinking. But the Buddha will, ultimately, lead them beyond this recognition.

The Parable of the Rain Cloud expresses this clearly:

> Like unto a great cloud the Tathagatha appears and sends forth his call to the whole world . . . lifts his voice and utters these words: 'I am the Tathagatha, O ye gods and men! The Arhat and the perfectly enlightened one; having reached the shore myself I carry others to the shore . . . . By my perfect wisdom I know both this world and the next as they really are. I am all-knowing, all-seeing . . . .
>
> I shall refresh all beings whose bodies are withered, who are clogged in the triple world.
>
> I shall bring to felicity those that are pining away with toils, give them pleasures and final rest.'
>
> So, it is the very nature of the law to promote the everlasting weal of the world; by the law the whole world is recreated, and as the plants, when refreshed, expand their blossoms, the world does the same when refreshed.
>
> So then, Kasyapa, is the preaching of the law, like the water poured out by the cloud everywhere alike; by which plants and men thrive, endless and eternal blossoms are produced.
>
> (Lotus Sutra 5)

The power of this poetic vision of a boundless creative and benevolent energy, producing creativity and happiness as it overcomes samsaric conditions by moving the world towards its final destiny, contrasts with the emphasis of the Theravadin teachings. Its liberating salvific message became the foundation of popular Buddhism across Northern Asia.

——— Pure Land Buddhism ———

When Buddhism reached China and Japan, two new schools of thought developed: the Pure Land School and the Ch'an (Chinese) or Zen (Japanese) School.

The two *Sukhavativyuha Sutras*, written in the second century CE, describe a Pure Land (*Sukhavati*) free from suffering. Sukhavati is a spiritual realm created by the Buddha, which is conducive to spiritual progress. It is a state of bliss (sukkha) and as such is the opposite of the samsaric realm we presently inhabit, which is marked by the pervasiveness of dukkha (unsatisfactoriness). The scriptures describe the Pure Land as, 'a world called Sukhavati where there is neither bodily or mental pain for living beings. The sources of happiness are innumerable.'

The *Sukhavativyuha Sutras* gave rise to a Buddhism of faith during the fifth and sixth centuries CE in China. It revolved around the Pure Land of Amitabha (Amida in Japanese) who is the Buddha of infinite Light and Compassion. To be reborn into his Pure Land, one only has to call his name ten times at the point of death and he will appear and escort his devotee to Sukhavati. Whilst in the present world gaining enlightenment is difficult, in death one will be helped on the path to that goal.

This is a Buddhism of Faith, in which the principal means of salvation is the invocation of the name of the Buddha, which will ensure attainment of a state from which there is no falling back. Its popularity was rooted in its ranking equally with more rigorous meditative practices and lifestyles through which wisdom was accomplished. For many lay Buddhists, especially those whose situations in life and possibilities of education were limited, this provided a suitable path. It also emphasised the Mahayanist teaching on the universality of salvation, because scholarly progress and monasticism were no longer required.

In the modern world this form of Buddhist practice is particularly stressed by the followers of Nichiren Daishonin, a Japanese master of the thirteenth century. He regarded the *Lotus Sutra* as the supreme teaching of the Buddha, and faith as the supreme attribute. Faith is increased by daily chanting of the *Gongyo*, the fruits of which are more positive energy and a deeper, more positive outlook as faith thereby increases. Chanting the mantra 'Nam – myoho – renge – kyo' assiduously and mindfully becomes a practice of purification, which will affect daily living and develop wisdom and compassion. In his teachings Nichiren Daishonin stated:

> The common mortal himself is the Buddha when he single-mindedly chants Nam-myoho-renge-kyo with strong faith. This is how he attains enlightenment naturally without discarding his life as a common mortal.
>
> (Honninnmyo Sho quoted in *'The Buddhism of the Sun'*, J. Cowan (ed) Nichiren Shoshu of the United Kingdom, 1982, p 78)

'Nam – myoho – renge – kyo' is rendered as 'devotion (*nam*) to the *Lotus Sutra*', the supreme law or all-embracing truth, which, by implication, is Buddhahood itself.

The Ch'an and Zen Schools

Ch'an (Chinese) and Zen (Japanese) are derived from the Indian word *dhyana*, which refers to meditation. As Buddhism extended into China, then Japan, so the meditation school developed from the teachings and practice of the sixth-century Indian monk, Bodhidharma. Ironically, Bodhidharma's message was that the tradition had become too attached to the scriptures, and that the Buddha's teaching was understood by simply watching the mind or looking into one's own heart (hence the emphasis on meditation, seen as a stripping away of external trappings). Such simplicity of expression was well-suited to a Chinese culture much influenced by Taoist philosophy, which also emphasised a one-pointedness of mind, a seeing to the heart of the matter within our everyday life but beyond our everyday understanding, as this verse illustrates:

> Thirty spokes
> Share one hub.

> Adapt the nothing therein to the purpose in hand, and you will have the use of the cart.
> Knead clay in order to make a vessel.

Adapt the nothing therein to the purpose in hand, and you will have the use of the vessel.

Cut out doors and windows in order to make a room.

Adapt the nothing therein to the purpose in hand, and you will have the use of the room.

Thus what we gain is Something, yet it is by virtue of Nothing that this can be put to use.

(Lao Tzu, *Tao Te Ching*, Penguin, 1968, p 67)

This represented a rigorous refusal to indulge in scriptural study or philosophical debate, in favour of a purely intuitive approach to enlightenment. Though the meditation school appeals to scripture to ground its practices in the authority of the Buddha, it does so only to support the efficacy of meditation as an end in itself, as the truth realised in action.

'Directly pointing to the mind' and 'becoming a Buddha just as you are', involves doing away with all thought, which is the means of attachment to the external world. The effect of this is to see into one's own Buddha-nature, which is obscured by defilements and attachments. Enlightenment may come suddenly or gradually. Either way, the intuiting of Truth involves the cultivation of the mind so that it is in sharp focus and constantly alert. Thus moments of pure awareness (*satori*) arise. As it developed, the meditation tradition identified Patriarchs, enlightened teachers who developed their own techniques for training their pupils and became founders of branches of the tradition. These techniques were often novel and unorthodox. For example, the followers of Lin-Chi used the 'lightning' method of scolding and beating disciples. Ts'ao-tung masters preferred the question-and-answer method, whereby the disciple would be interviewed by his master to test his capacity to intuit the truth.

The story of the enlightenment of the sixth patriarch, Hui-Neng, illustrates the character of Ch'an teaching well.

Hui-Neng: The Sixth Patriarch

One day the Fifth Patriarch (Hung-jen) suddenly called all his pupils to come to him. As they assembled, he said, 'Let me say this to you. Birth and death are serious matters. You people are engaged all day in making offerings (to the Buddha), going after blessings and rewards only, and you make no effort to achieve freedom from the bitter sea of life and death. Your self-nature seems to be obscured. How can blessings save you? Go to your rooms and examine yourselves. He who is enlightened use his perfect vision of self-nature and write me a verse. When I look at his verse, if it reveals deep understanding, I shall give him the robe and the Law and make him the Sixth Patriarch. Hurry, hurry!'

At midnight Shen-hsui, holding a candle, wrote a verse on the wall of the south corridor, without anyone knowing about it, which said:

> Our body is the tree of Perfect Wisdom,
> And our mind is a bright mirror.
> At all times diligently wipe them,
> So that they will be free from dust.

The Fifth Patriarch said: 'The verse you wrote shows some but not all understanding. You have arrived at the front of the door but you have not yet entered it. Ordinary people, by practising in accordance with your verse, will not degenerate. But it will be futile to seek the Supreme Perfect Wisdom while holding to such a view. One must enter the door and see his self-nature. Go away and come back after one or two days of thought. If you have entered the door and seen your self-nature, I shall give you the robe and the Law.'

Shen-hsui went away and for several days could not produce another verse.

Hui-neng also wrote a verse . . . which said:

> The tree of Perfect Wisdom is originally no tree.
> Nor has the bright mirror any frame.
> Buddha-nature is forever clear and pure.
> Where is there any dust?

and another verse:

> The mind is the tree of Perfect Wisdom.
> The body is the clear mirror.
> The clear mirror is originally clear and pure.
> Where has it been affected by any dust?

Monks in the hall were all surprised at these verses. Hui-neng, however, went back to the rice-pounding room. The Fifth Patriarch suddenly realised that Hui-neng was the one of good knowledge but was afraid lest the rest learn it. He therefore told them: 'This will not do.'

The Fifth Patriarch waited till midnight, called Hui-neng to come to the hall, and expounded the Diamond Sutra. As soon as Hui-neng heard this, he understood. That night the Law was imparted to him without anyone knowing it, and thus the Law and the robe of Sudden Enlightenment were transmitted to him. 'You are now the Sixth Patriarch,' said the Fifth Patriarch to Hui-neng. 'The robe is the testimony of transmission from generation to generation. As to the Law, it is to be transmitted from mind to mind. Let people achieve understanding through their own effort.'

(Wm. Theodore De Barry (ed), *Sources of Chinese Tradition*, Columbia University Press, 1960, p 350)

Characteristic of Zen is the refusal to give 'right answers', as though truth can be passed on just by hearing or reading a teaching. The master's skill lies in knowing exactly what the disciple requires to free his mind from attachment. Attachment may come in many forms and the mind can be freed from particular attachments in many ways. Zen stories (*Mondos*) catalogue this highly practical method of teaching.

Here are two examples:

A Cup of Tea

Nan-in, a Japanese master during the Meiji era, (1868–1912), received a university professor who came to inquire about Zen. Nan-in served tea. He poured his visitor's cup full, and then kept on pouring. The professor watched the overflow until he no longer could restrain himself. 'It is overfull. No more will go in!' 'Like this cup,' Nan-in said, 'you are full of your own opinions and speculations. How can I show you Zen unless you first empty your cup?'

(P. Reps, *Zen Flesh, Zen Bones*, Pelican, 1972, p 17)

Happy Chinaman

Anyone walking about Chinatowns in America will observe statues of a stout fellow carrying a linen sack. Chinese merchants call him Happy Chinaman or Laughing Buddha.

This Hotei lived in the T'ang dynasty. He had no desire to call himself a Zen master or to gather many disciples about him. Instead he walked the streets with a big sack into which he would put gifts of candy, fruit, or doughnuts. These he would give to children who gathered around him in play. He established a kindergarten of the streets.

Whenever he met a Zen devotee he would extend his hand and say, 'Give me one penny.' And if anyone asked him to return to a temple to teach others, again he would reply: 'Give me one penny.'

Once as he was about his play-work another Zen master happened along and inquired: 'What is the significance of Zen?'
Hotei immediately plopped his sack down on the ground in silent answer.

'Then,' asked the other, 'what is the actualization of Zen?'

At once the Happy Chinaman swung the sack over his shoulder and continued on his way.

(P. Reps, *Zen Flesh, Zen Bones*, Pelican, 1972, p 27)

The following story illustrates a particularly famous Zen technique, know as the *Koan*, which is given to stop the discriminating mind with its reliance on intellectual understanding.

The Sound of One Hand

The master of Kennin temple was Mokurai, Silent Thunder. He had a little protege named Toyo who was only twelve years old. Toyo saw the older disciples visit the master's room each morning and evening to receive instructions in *sanzen,* or personal guidance, in which they were given koans to stop mind-wandering.

Toyo wished to do sanzen also. 'Wait a while,' said Mokurai. 'You are too young.'

But the child insisted, so the teacher finally consented.

In the evening little Toyo went at the proper time to the threshold of Mokurai's sanzen room. He struck the gong to announce his presence, bowed respectfully three times outside the door, and went to sit before the master in respectful silence.

'You can hear the sound of two hands when they clap together,' said Mokurai. 'Now show me the sound of one hand.'

Toyo bowed and went to his room to consider this problem. From his window he could hear the music of the geishas. 'Ah, I have it!' he proclaimed.

The next evening, when his teacher asked him to illustrate the sound of one hand, Toyo began to play the music of the geishas.

'No, no,' said Mokurai. 'That will never do. That is not the sound of one hand. You've not got it at all.'

Thinking that such music might interrupt, Toyo moved his abode to a quiet place. He meditated again. 'What can the sound of one hand be?' He happened to hear some water dripping. 'I have it,' imagined Toyo.

When he next appeared before his teacher, Toyo imitated dripping water.

'What is that?' asked Mokurai. 'That is the sound of dripping water, but not the sound of one hand. Try again.'

In vain Toyo meditated to hear the sound of one hand. He heard the sighing of the wind. But the sound was rejected. He heard the cry of an owl. This also was refused. The sound of one hand was not the locusts.

For more than ten times Toyo visited Mokurai with different sounds. All were wrong. For almost a year he pondered what the sound of one hand might be.

At last little Toyo entered true meditation and transcended all sounds. 'I could collect no more,' he explained later, 'so I reached the soundless sound.'

Toyo had realized the sound of one hand.

(P. Reps, *Zen Flesh*, *Zen Bones*, Pelican, 1972, pp 34–35)

Rinzai and Soto Zen

The branches into which Zen split, the Rinzai and Soto Zen, emphasised the koan and silent sitting respectively, as techniques for attaining this 'pure seeing' into the true nature of things. Nevertheless, these two schools are not entirely distinct in their practices. As one writer has observed:

> In the Rinzai sect we find the dynamic character of the daring koan experiment and of lightning-like enlightenment, while the Soto School is characterised by a preference for silent sitting in zazen and the quiet deeds of everyday life . . . It appears (in Japan) . . . that adherence to one sect or the other is determined largely by the spiritual bent of the monks, who are inherently suited to one tradition or the other and pursue enlightenment in a way appropriate to their character. Thus one can find in the temples of the Soto sect men of brilliant wit and dynamic char-

acter who devote themselves to the koan exercises, while on the other hand certain Rinzai monks of subdued character can scarcely be distinguished from Soto disciples.

(N. Wilson Ross, *Hinduism*, *Buddhism*, *Zen*, Faber and Faber, 1973, p 156)

Zen cultural life

Japanese culture has been greatly influenced by Zen Buddhism. Its techniques pervade such arts and skills as flower-arranging and archery, as well as being the foundation of traditional ceremonies, most famously the Tea Ceremony. In literature it gave birth to the Haiku, the seventeen-syllable poem that points to the Buddha-nature, or pure-reality, being everywhere in the here and now. It illustrates the typically Zen emphasis on the paradox that the everyday and the wonder of enlightenment are but one and the same thing.

> How marvellous, how miraculous,
> I draw water
> I carry fuel.

———— The Tibetan Scriptures ————

Buddhism entered Tibet around 650 BCE, but it was not until a century later that it overcame fierce resistance from the indigenous Bon religion, with its shamanic heritage and patronage of the Tibetan nobility. As so often with religious incursion, it was the support of rulership that caused changes in fortune. This was true of the spread of Christianity within the Roman world, under the reign of the emperor Constantine, and the proliferation of Buddhism in India under the emperor Ashoka. So in Tibet, once patronage moved from Bon to Buddhism, it flourished under the reign of Ral-pa-can (817-36 CE). Monasteries and temples were erected, and teachers were brought from India, which propagated the translation of the scriptures.

The relationship with the Bon tradition was not wholly one of animosity, and Padmasambhava, one of the most revered of Tibetan saints, did much as an Indian missionary to realign hostile forces, through his particular interpretation of practices and teachings. Buddhism also entered Tibet from China, though its impact was less successful; the character of Tibetan Buddhism illustrates Indian influence rather than Chinese.

It should also be noted that relations between Tibet and China have generally been full of unease, due to Chinese imperialism, which has resurfaced today in the annexing of Tibet and the exile of the Dalai Lama, Head of both Church and State in Tibet.

Tibet has largely been isolated as a kingdom and culture over the majority of its history, and this has been both a blessing and a curse from the Buddhist point of view. The blessing is that it was able to preserve and develop the Mahayana teachings in a distinctive way over one thousand years, with little interference. Indeed, it became recognised as a secret kingdom, seen as the repository of Buddhist wisdom by many westerners, and this was the subject of various forms of pilgrimage in the early part of the twentieth century. Westerners who came to Tibet included Heinrich Harrer, the German prisoner of war who wrote *Seven Years in Tibet*; Alexandra David-Neel, who wrote *With Mystics and Magicians in Tibet* and W.Y. Evans Wentz who translated *The Tibetan Book of the Dead*.

The drawback was that such distinctive and ancient teachings as Tibet possessed (along with the traditions and schools which progressed from them) did not become known to the outside world until the Chinese invasion in 1959, and the subsequent dispersion of Lamas and teachers to India and the West. Today there are western scholars working with Tibetan teachers, to make known the teachings and practices which had been preserved in Tibet.

There are four main Tibetan traditions alive today: the Nyingma, Kagya, Sakya and Geluk, each of which possess a wealth of oral and written teachings. The scriptures are classified under the following titles: The *Kangyur*, meaning 'the translation of the word', which are discourses attributed to the historical Buddha; and the *Tengyur*, which are the *shastras* (commentaries on the original teachings, translated from Indian originals). In addition to these, numerous explanatory works were written in Tibetan.

The importance of Tibetan Buddhism and its scriptures is not so much that it is specifically Tibetan, but that a great deal of the corpus of Mahayana Buddhist literature, and the maintenance of its tradition, would not have survived had it not been harboured in Tibet.

Tibetan scriptures and practices can appear obscure to uninitiated westerners; this is not surprising given its isolated history. But one of the principal emphases that underlie its tradition is the need to learn from an enlightened teacher. As one western Tibetan Buddhist writes:

> Lost in the middle of a dense, dark forest, drowning in a wild and savage sea, locked in chains in a lonely dungeon, we rely on the wisdom, power and compassion of those who can set us free. To escape from the stifling darkness of ignorance, from the raging tides of the delusions, from the iron chains of karma, we must turn to an enlightened guide. Since we need a qualified teacher to learn such simple skills as reading, writing and mathematics, how can we think to travel the long and difficult path of Dharma alone? It is absolutely essential to follow a spiritual master who has passed that way himself. Finding the right spiritual master is the most important thing in life; following him correctly is the root of the path to enlightenment.
>
> (Nicholas Ribush, 'A Profile of Tibetan Buddhism', in P. Connolly and C. Erricker: *The Presence and Practice of Buddhism*, West Sussex Institute of Higher Education, 1985, p 72)

Another preoccupation of Tibetan teaching is the relationship between life and death. This arises mainly due to the significance of Tantric teaching in Tibetan tradition. *Tantra* represents the quick path to enlightenment in one lifetime, by grasping the opportunity of a human birth not to be wasted. It also stresses the importance of confronting our negative impulses and fears during this rebirth. Death is seen as the ultimate fear or barrier, because it represents an annihilation of our identity (as we perceive it). *The Tibetan Book of the Dead* attains an especial importance, since it deals with how to find our way through the period between death and rebirth. This concept is referred to as the 'Art of Dying', which is seen as the most significant liberating experience in Tibetan Buddhist terms.

The Tibetans understand there to be a state between dying and being reborn, referred to as the *Bardo* state. During this time the individual will follow a course that leads to liberation or a consequent rebirth according to his or her attachments. This journey is dependent on our last thoughts in our present life, and the course that they initiate, rather like a train of thought that is pursued, from its inception in thinking about either positive or negative impulses (for example, a day when we wake up with a negative or positive frame of mind). It is claimed that reading *The Tibetan Book of the Dead* to a dying person will initiate them into the process of dying in a positive frame of mind, and therefore ensure either a positive rebirth or freedom from rebirth entirely. Aldous Huxley is one westerner who adhered to this philosophy and followed its practice, despite the adverse criticism that ensued from the American press and subsequent biographies.

The Buddhist rationale for such a practice is that our past thinking has determined our present status, and our present thinking will determine our future status. This is rooted in scriptural understanding and the significance of karmic influence. What *The Tibetan Book of the Dead* (*Bardo Thodol*) points to is the most significant event in our lives – our own demise – for which we have a whole lifetime either to prepare for or to ignore. It indicates the importance of preparation for the ultimate test of our earthly achievement, when all else that we rely on has passed: status, reputation and other worldly successes. We are left only with our own mind, naked and unprotected. At this point the practice of the teaching bears fruit:

> O now when the Dhyana Bardo upon me is dawning!
> Abandoning the whole mass of distractions and illusions,
> May the mind be kept in the mood of endless undistracted Samadhi,
> May firmness both in the visualizing and in the perfected stages be obtained:
> At this time, when meditating one-pointedly, with all other actions put aside,
> May I not fall under the power of misleading, stupifying passions.
> (W.Y. Evans-Wentz, *The Tibetan Book of the Dead*, Oxford University Press, 1960, p 203)

5
MEDITATION AND DEVOTION

Once, when talking to a friend about the possibility of him moving to a new place and starting a new business, I asked him whether he thought it would be good for him to make a fresh start. He replied that he had done enough travelling in his life to know that wherever you go, deep down there is no such thing as a fresh start: you take yourself and your hang-ups with you. I was looking on the outside and he was looking on the inside. My understanding of the situation was relatively superficial; his was much more profound.

Most of the time we think of the world being outside ourselves. This is the place where our actions have their effect and changes occur. If we want the world to be a better place, we have to influence it in a moral way, to create greater harmony and better communication. For Buddhists, like everyone else, this is a worthy goal; the question is, how do we achieve it? For followers of a monotheistic faith, such as Christianity, Judaism or Islam, the spiritual power for change comes from God through prayer. For Buddhists it occurs through training the mind, and recognising our true nature.

Training the mind

However, to understand this Buddhist notion of self-transformation, our conception of 'mind' has to be freed from its western connotations. Within Indian tradition, 'mind' and 'heart' are both aspects of consciousness, and the practice of meditation, with its yogic origins, both presumes this and is the way to realising it.

The Buddha's path is simple and meant for ordinary people, and anyone with goodwill and determination can follow its steps toward freedom of heart and mind. Both heart and mind have to be involved in this journey toward liberation from the 'self'. The mind understands and concludes, connects and discerns, whereas the heart feels.

(Ayya Keema, *Being Nobody, Going Nowhere*,
Wisdom Publications, 1987, preface)

For this reason, the words heart and mind are often used interchangeably to refer to our inner world, which we need to purify through the cultivation of mindfulness. The Buddha said:

'O Bhikkhus, there are two kinds of illness. What are these two? Physical illness and mental illness. There seem to be people who enjoy freedom from physical illness even for a year or two . . . even for a hundred years or more. But, O Bhikkus, rare in this world are those who enjoy freedom from mental illness even for one moment, except those who are free from mental defilements.
(Anguttara Nikaya, Devamitta Thera (ed.), Colombo, 1929, p 276)

Here mental illness is not contrasted with an ordinary or 'normal' state of mind, but with the perfectly healthy or pure mind of one who has overcome suffering and dis-ease (an Arahant). Mental defilements, which prevent this liberation, are not simply clinical conditions, but the result of a mind that is untrained and unrestrained, not functioning according to its true nature and therefore preventing happiness, contentment, tranquillity. This training of the mind is referred to in one famous Zen text as *The Taming of the Bull*. It begins with *The Search for the Bull*:

In the pasture of this world, I endlessly push aside the tall grasses in search of the bull.
Following unnamed rivers, lost upon the interpenetrating paths of distant mountains,
My strength failing and my vitality exhausted, I cannot find the bull.
I only hear the locusts chirring through the forest at night.

Following the verse is a comment:

The bull has been lost. What need is there to search? Only because of separation from my true nature, I fail to find him. In

the confusion of the senses I lose even his tracks. Far from
home, I see many crossroads, but which way is the right one I
know not. Greed and fear, good and bad, entangle me.

(P. Reps, *Zen Flesh, Zen Bones*, Penguin, 1972, p 138)

Eventually the bull is tamed, and it is realised that it was nothing
more than the restless activity of the 'self'. With the self now eradicated,
Wisdom and Compassion arise, and attachment ceases:

Barefoot and naked of breast, I mingle with the people of the
world.
My clothes are ragged and dust-laden and I am ever-blissful.
I use no magic to extend my life;
Now, before me, the trees become alive.

(ibid., p 147)

Ethical considerations are also integral to the attainment of this
healthy state, since a healthy or pure mind functions according to
selfless motivation, rather than through the pursuit of egotistical
goals. When we put these aspects of the Buddhist analysis of mind
together, we find they are summed up in the Eightfold Path: wisdom,
morality and mental discipline. Bhavana (mental development) or
meditation is the basis of living a Buddhist way of life.

Mindfulness and concentration

Ayya Khema, a Buddhist nun, writes:

During meditation we learn to drop from the mind what we
don't want to keep. We only want to keep in mind our meditation subject. As we become more and more skilled at it, we start
to use the same faculty in our daily lives to help us drop those
thoughts which are unwholesome. In this way our meditation
practice assists us in daily living and our attention to wholesome thoughts in everyday life helps our meditation practice.
The person who becomes master of his or her own thoughts and
learns to think what they want to think is called an Arahant, an
Enlightened One.

(Ayya Khema, *Being Nobody, Going Nowhere*,
Wisdom Publications, 1987, p 11)

Formal meditation practice is like exercising the mind in the same
way as we might exercise the body – in order to keep it fit and

healthy, and to improve its function for a specific purpose. The basic function of the mind is concentration. Right Concentration is the eighth step of the path, but this does not mean it is the one which comes last. Rather, we have to think of the eight steps as the development of skilfulness in eight aspects which go hand in hand, like a progressive and interdependent evolution. Most importantly, without Right Concentration, Right Mindfulness is unattainable. Thus basic exercises of concentration are the foundation of meditation. But concentration on what? The most widely used traditional practice is called mindfulness of, or concentration on, breathing (*anapanasati*).

Mindfulness of the breath

The breath is a good focus for such a meditational exercise because it is neutral. As a bodily function it usually escapes our attention, since it does not give rise to pleasant or unpleasant sensations, nor does it excite the mind. Because we take it for granted we also overlook its significance, in much the same way as we do with a life-giving substance like water. Yet it is the basis of life. Equally, its relationship with the mind is direct in a physiological and emotional sense. Breath provides oxygen, through which the mind functions. In a state of excitement we breathe fast; in a state of calm and tranquillity we breathe slowly. The breath is therefore an indicator of our mental state.

We can concentrate on the breath at various points: as it goes into and exits from the body, by concentrating on the sensation of it passing through the nostrils; by following its passage down to and returning from the abdomen; by accompanying each breath cycle with a word, such as 'Buddho' (a reminder of the relationship between concentration and enlightenment); by counting breaths, one on the in-breath, two on the out-breath, and so on up to ten.

The point is to know when concentration is focused and refined, and when the mind wanders and concentration is lost. It is important to make the distinction between the discipline of concentration and 'just thinking about something'. When the mind wanders, thoughts are arising but we are not aware of them. Concentration is a full awareness of exactly what is happening here and now, which is why it requires a discipline that thinking alone does not possess. To start with, counting is a good way to ensure you obey this distinction. If the mind wanders you may forget to count altogether, or count beyond the number at which you should return to one. Realising you have done this is evidence of the mind having wandered. As the practice progresses, concentration should increase. It is then you begin to realise how subtle concentration can be, and how easily it can be lost. You will also realise how an excited mind finds it difficult to concentrate, and strays to objects of desire, or becomes distracted by dominant feelings. This is the learning process of meditation, which can be both frustrating and irritating. Feelings arise which are distracting, and which give rise to impatience, anger and frustration. The most simple exercise can be a humbling experience. After all, if this simple activity presents problems in a relaxed environment, how much more difficult would concentration be in the more rapid and distracting context of our everyday life?

With increasing concentration the mind becomes more tranquil, and its activity diminishes. In a state of pure calm, an awareness arises of the present moment that is undisturbed, and with it arises a moment of bliss, a lack of anxiety. When the mind is in this state, its energy is available for the purposes for which we choose to use it, unhampered by negative feelings.

Ayya Khema describes such a condition in this way:

> Once verbalisation stops for a moment, not only is there quiet but there is a feeling of contentment. The mind has at last found its home. We wouldn't be very happy if we didn't have a home for this body of ours. We are equally not very happy if we haven't got a home for the mind. That quiet, peaceful space is the mind's home. It can go home and relax just as we do after a day's work when we relax the body in an easy chair and at night in bed. Now the mind, too, can take it easy. It doesn't have to think. Thinking is suffering, no matter what it is that we think. There is movement in it and because of that there is friction. Everything that moves creates friction.
>
> The moment we relax and rest the mind it gains new strength and also happiness because it knows it can go home at any time. The happiness created at the time of meditation carries through to daily living because the mind knows that nothing has to be taken so seriously that it can't go home again and find peace and quiet.

(ibid., pp 13–14)

Calm and insight

Insight is the goal; calm is the means. Many images have been used to illustrate this. One is of the sea, both in its calm state and in a storm. The calm sea is tranquil and serene, not only in itself, but in the effect it has upon us. Similarly, waves, foam and the sea's roar in a storm are exciting, powerful and fearful. The calm sea is like the calm mind. The stormy sea is a mind in turmoil. When the sea is calm we can see through it, but in its rough state, nothing below the surface can be seen. This ability to see below the surface is insight. We see with clarity and penetration. There is a picture by the Japanese artist Hokusai, called *The Waves at Kanagawa*. It depicts

The Waves at Kanagawa, Hokusai

figures in small boats confronted by a huge wave, its aggressive shape about to bear down on them. They are cowering on the deck in fear. In the distance, unnoticed, and difficult to pick out in the picture, is Mount Fuji, the symbol of enlightenment in Japanese Buddhism. Its snow-capped peak resembles the waves that frame it. Reading this picture, like a Zen *mondo*, or story, the figures confronted with their fear of the wave and their death are forgetful of the path to enlightenment. Their mindfulness is distracted by the sensations of the moment. The wave may represent any fearful circumstance we face, but the message is clear. Without preparing for such moments in our life – even death itself – we shall be lost in samsara when they come. Insight is the antidote to such situations, and meditation is the way to cultivate it.

Meditational techniques

Accordingly, meditational techniques are divided into two types: *samatha*, which means calm; and *vipassana*, which means insight. Insight means knowing what is really happening in our minds and in our relations with others, and doing our best to create a harmonious situation in every circumstance. The significance of insight may best be described by showing how it can be obscured by negative feelings arising in the present moment. I come to each situation in a particular state of mind. Sometimes, when depressed, sad or sorrowful, I greet people in this particular state, and it colours my impression of them and the way I feel about them. This is essentially a preoccupation with myself that interferes with my concern for others and their well-being, but I say, 'I cannot help it'. Such states can be self-perpetuating and gather momentum. In my morose condition, the happy person is someone to be envied. I cannot share in their happiness and, inevitably, this shows. Then I complain about losing friends or not being wanted, and the downward spiral continues. If someone says, 'cheer up', or, 'it is not as bad as it seems', I feel even worse! Insight is the recognition of what is going on in our minds when these feelings arise, so that we may prevent ourselves from slipping back into similar mental habits time and time again. Mindfulness creates the opportunity to change these habits, by letting go of our attachment to them.

The first step on this path is to recognise such thoughts and feelings as delusion. Not because they do not exist, but because they do not constitute our 'selves'. They are not 'me', but phenomena which arise and pass away. This is the truth of impermanence that vipassana meditation makes clear. Nothing abides, nothing has to be held onto. Without this awareness the mind manipulates us, like a magician, into believing the illusions that our thoughts convey; these illusions in turn cause us distress and separate us from others.

For this reason, every sensation is a matter for awareness: those of the body, and feelings and thoughts. The contemplation of the six elements is an example of this reflection on impermanence.

The contemplation of the six elements

One considers the solid matter of the body: bones, hair, skin, nails, flesh and so on. These are the earth elements. When one dies they return to the earth elements in the universe. They are only borrowed, not one's own.

One considers the liquid elements in the body: blood, phlegm, bile and other secretions. These are the water elements. One therefore reflects, they too are not one's own.

One considers the fire element within the body: heat and energy.

One considers the air element: breath and wind.

These elements are also borrowed and will return. They are not one's own.

One considers that the space the body occupies will also be surrendered at death.

Lastly, even individual consciousness will also have to be given up at death. Each of the six elements that make up the body (earth, water, fire, air, space and consciousness) are not permanent and abiding as one's own body. Upon recognition of this, attachment to one's own body will slip away as insight increases.

Similar reflections on feelings, mind and other objects are used to the same effect; not as a means of morose introspection, but to remove attachment to that which is not abiding and untrustworthy – and, therefore, ultimately, the cause of sorrow, delusion and self-concern. As this decreases, so one's burden is lightened and Right Understanding increases.

Metta

Another important Buddhist teaching is that one should be a blessing to the world. There is a Zen picture of a Bodhisattva, who wanders with his staff visiting villages, depicted standing smiling with children around him. The legend that accompanies the picture explains that he enters the village with bliss-bestowing hands. This expresses the purpose of what is aspired to in the Buddhist life.

Metta is the word that sums up this state of being. The *Metta-sutta*, the teaching on universal love or loving-kindness, proclaims that:

Whatever beings there may be – feeble or strong, long (or tall), stout or medium or short, small or large, seen or unseen, those dwelling far or near, those who are born and those who are yet to be born – may all beings, without exception, be happy-minded.

Mettabhavana

This undiscriminating attitude is cultivated in a popular meditation (*mettabhavana*). It consists of five stages. In the first one generates metta for oneself. (This is not a self-love in the sense of self-appreciation as a special person, above others, but a recognition of one's capacity to be loving to others and loveable.) At this stage one repeats: 'May I be well, may I be happy, may I progress.' In the second stage the feeling is extended to a friend. In the third stage to a neutral person. In the fourth to someone towards whom you have antipathy. In the fifth you see all these together, and then visualise the whole world of living beings and extend metta to all of them.

Thus, what appears at first to be an easy practice becomes progressively more difficult, proceeding through the stages: it confronts limitations rather than indulging preferences. As such, it also distinguishes between the notion of love which we may find appealing, and that which is demanded of us. The highest aspiration mentioned in the teaching on loving kindness is that one should love all beings just as a mother loves her child, or, alternatively, that one should see all beings as having been, at one time, one's mother. It is not a soft option, and requires much work in the training of the heart. Most importantly, it is a progressive insight into the true meaning of love and the demands which that makes. It is the path to compassion, which is often spoken of as consisting of three grades. The first grade consists of goodwill towards others. The second is friendship. The third stage, metta itself, lies beyond these and is not just an emotion but a developed skill, which progressively exposes our own weakness and vulnerability. It also has its benefits, of course. If we offer goodwill, friendship or love to others, they will feel attracted to us. But love is given not because we want to give something, or because they need it, but because the heart has been trained to do it. In other words, in time, it becomes a *spontaneous* giving rather than a difficulty. The formal practice of mettabhavana is a training for our motivation in ordinary circumstances: at home, at work and in the supermarket.

Visualisation

The skill of visualisation is a way both of concentrating the mind and of developing the quality of compassion. One Buddhist writer explains:

> For our efforts at the spiritual life to be crowned with success not only do we need to be intellectually convinced by Buddhism, but we also need to find it emotionally attractive. We need both Truth and Beauty. Images, especially beautiful images, involve our emotions in the spiritual life and thereby make it possible for us actually to live it.
>
> (*FWBO Newsletter*, No 56, 1982, p 12)

Visualisation is not just a development of our imagination, but a focusing of our inherent qualities for transforming ourselves and the world, through 'seeing with the mind's eye'. It emancipates us from the effect of negative emotions, thus enabling us to respond more effectively to difficult situations that we encounter. Essentially, it means that by visualising the form of a Bodhisattva (a being with higher qualities), we let go of our egotistical desires and our selfhood, and are therefore able to act in the world in a more beneficial way.

Kuan Yin

This example shows the process by which it can occur. The focus of the visualisation is Kuan Yin, the Chinese form of the Bodhisattva of Compassion.

You sit down on a hill top, or anywhere high enough for you to
see nothing but the sky in front of your eyes
With your mind you make everything empty.

There is nothing there you say.
And you see it like that – nothing
emptiness.
Then you say ahhh.....

But there is something!
Look there's the sea
and the MOON has risen
full, round, white.

And you see it like that
sea, silver in the moonlight
with little white topped waves.
And in the blue black sky above
hangs a great moon
bright,
but not dazzling,
a soft brightness you might say.

You stare at the moon a long
long time, feeling calm, happy.
Then the moon gets smaller,
but brighter and brighter and brighter
till you see it as a pearl, or a seed, but not so bright
you can only just bear to look at it.

The pearl starts to grow.
And before you know what's happened,
it's Kuan Yin (the Mother of Compassion) herself
standing up against the sky
all dressed in gleaming white
and with her feet resting on a lotus
that floats on the waves.

You see her
once you know how to do it
as clearly as I see you.
For her robes are shining,
and there's a halo round her head.
She smiles at you,
such a loving smile. She's so glad
to see you that tears of happiness sparkle in her eyes.

If you keep your mind calm,
by just whispering her name
and not trying too hard
she will stay a long time.

When she does go,
it's by getting smaller and smaller.
She doesn't go back to being a pearl,
but just gets so small
that at last you can't see her, then you notice
that the sky and the sea
have vanished too.
Just space is left.
Lovely, lovely space, going on forever . . .

that space stays long
if you can do without you. Not you and space, you see
just space.

No you!

Bowing to the Buddha

It is commonly assumed that Buddhism has nothing to do with devotion because it is concerned with self-transformation. It is also assumed that devotion presumes an outside power or agency to which we submit. For these reasons, Buddhist ritual appears anachronistic.

Yet there is no more pervasive devotional action performed by Buddhists than bowing, which is apparently an act of worship and submission. What lies behind this activity?

Buddhists participate in *pujas*, which is an Indian word for formal worship. It is rather like Christians attending a church service. When Buddhists enter a temple or shrine room in which an image of a Buddha is installed, they may go before the image, kneel down and bow three times so that their forehead touches the floor. This is a very formal action. The three bows represent the Buddha, Dhamma and Sangha.

Tibetan Buddhists often prostrate themselves (an extension of bowing), by lying full length on the floor with the head pointing towards the image. There is no denying that this is an act of devotion, but it is not to be confused with worship shown towards God. Such a ritual (rather like the act of offering flowers, candles and incense which are traditional Buddhist offerings) acts as a reminder of commitment to an ideal, and a way of bringing oneself closer to that ideal. The whole person has to be engaged in this act of transformation and piety. Expressed in these forms, bowing is a means to this transformation, just as much as solitary meditation and ethical action in the world. Mindfulness is cultivated by expression of devotion as much as by these other activities. It forms part of the training of the heart, in which the emotions are touched, and the development of qualities like humility, upon which the aspiration to Buddhahood and a better life depend. When Buddhists bow or make offerings, they should genuinely recognise that they aspire to progress by recognising that the ideal lies beyond them in the present, but that it is attainable. Acts of devotion express a determination to develop the qualities embodied by the venerated image. The offerings of candles, flowers and incense express gratitude and reverence but do not imply 'otherness' (in the sense of Christian devotion to an Almighty but essentially distinct God). Flowers are a reminder of beauty and impermanence. The candles are a reminder of the light of the Dhamma in the darkness of ignorance. The fragrance of incense is a reminder of the blessing of compassionate service.

In *pujas* (formal acts of worship), these offerings are accompanied by chanting, which recollects the meaning and purpose of the devotion. Here are two examples. The first is from the Thai Forest Retreat Order, established in England by Ajahn Chah, the Thai meditation master:

To the Blessed One, the Lord who fully attained perfect enlightenment,
To the Teaching which he expounded so well,
And to the Blessed One's disciples, who have practised well,
To these – the Buddha, the Dhamma and the Sangha –
We render with offerings our rightful homage.
It is well for us, Blessed One, that having attained liberation,
You still had compassion for later generations.
Deign to accept these simple offerings
For our long-lasting benefit and for the happiness it gives us.
The Lord, the Perfectly Enlightened and Blessed One –
I render homage to the Buddha, the Blessed One.
    (*Amaravati Chanting Book*, Amaravati Publications, 1987, p 9)

The second is from the *Friends of the Western Buddhist Order Puja*.

Offerings to the Buddha.
Reverencing the Buddha, we offer flowers –
Flowers that today are fresh and sweetly blooming,
Flowers that tomorrow are faded and fallen.
Our bodies too, like flowers, will pass away.

Reverencing the Buddha, we offer candles.

To Him, who is the Light, we offer light.
From His greater lamp a lesser lamp we light within us:
The lamp of Bodhi shining within our hearts.

Reverencing the Buddha, we offer incense,
Incense whose fragrance pervades the air.
The fragrance of the perfect life, sweeter than incense,
Spreads in all directions throughout the world.
            (*FWBO Puja Book*, Windhorse Publications)

Bowing to the Buddha, making offerings and chanting constitute the three main acts of Buddhist devotion, or puja ceremonies. They take place before a shrine – which may vary in style according to the branch of the tradition, but the intention is always the same. This quotation, taken from the short ceremony for the dedication of a shrine room in the Friends of the Western Buddhist Order (a Western Buddhist movement), succinctly sums up the purpose of shrine room and ceremony:

Here seated, here practising,
May our mind become Buddha,
May our thought become Dharma,
May our communication with one another be Sangha.

(FWBO Puja Book, Windhorse Publications)

So we may conclude that mind and heart, meditation and devotion, are complementary aspects of the same training in bhavana, or mental development. This training is essentially practical, not simply intellectual, nor ethereal. It is creative in that it aims to ensure a better world through self-transformation and, ultimately, the transformation of the world itself.

Tibetan women showing devotion before the Temple at Dharamsala, India. (Copyright Peter Gold. Photograph reproduced from *Tibetan Reflections* with permission from Wisdom Publications, 361 Newbury Street, Boston, Massachusetts, USA.

6
ETHICAL
CONDUCT

Sila and skilfulness

Sila is the Buddhist term for ethical or moral behaviour, which is summed up in the three connected ethical steps of the Eightfold Path (Right Speech, Right Action, Right Livelihood, referred to in Chapter 3). At the same time, an emphasis on living well pervades Buddhist teaching and practice. This is expressed in an obvious way, in the precepts which provide everyday guidance in a simple form (simple to remember, that is, rather than simple to keep). But in order to keep the precepts successfully, Buddhists recognise the need for sustained development in themselves. We could say that the precepts provide a practical framework, for us to be guided by in our everyday activity, but the intention is to try to keep them. This intention and effort are all-important, otherwise no progress can be made. Behind the precepts encompassing them is the Eightfold Path, which informs Buddhists as to how this can be achieved. Bhavana, or mental development, is what lies beneath the surface, what is happening within the person that creates this possibility. The aspiration at the heart of this is skilfulness, its effect in the world and on others, is the cultivation of happiness and harmony.

Perhaps we can best illustrate this by returning to the physician or doctor analogy that was applied by the Buddha himself. First, there is the problem: we do not achieve in life what we wish to achieve. Our aspirations toward happiness are not fulfilled. Why is this? The prescription is that we have to reflect carefully on how we can best achieve what it is that we seek, and why we seek it. This, however, turns out to be a long-term task. It involves recognising why we suffer the dissatisfaction we experience, and, in the course of this, through meditation and mindfulness, how we can alter our way of responding to life (which, at root, means recognising that what we think and do isn't necessarily good for us or anyone else). Here the doctor prescribes a sustained programme that should result in a cure for the illness. This is laid out in the Eightfold Path. At the same time, we need some everyday guidance as to what we should and should not do; some rules to try to keep that will be easy to remember to keep us on track in the hurly-burly of our life, when our desires are likely to be least restrained. This is the purpose of the precepts. Similarly, the good doctor will be concerned with the root causes of our lack of health, and give us a checklist of things to do and not to do day by day. These two aspects of treating the situation go hand in hand, complementing each other. But it would be a mistake to think we could just try and follow the rules and everything would be sorted out.

Let us take a specific example. I hurt my leg badly, sustaining an injury that will take quite a while to mend. The rules are to rest, not do anything that will hamper recovery such as twisting, bending or running. At the same time, my leg will lose its strength unless I make sure that the path to recovery also includes building up the muscles, ligaments and so forth, at an appropriate time. If I carry out the first instructions as best I can but ignore the second, my leg will always be weak and liable to further injury. At the same time, I shall be unlikely ever to be able to do after the injury what I could have done previously.

The analogy ends here, because the Buddha was not concerned with rehabilitation but with improvement. Neither was he concerned with a purely physical condition, but with what we might call a spiritual one. The root of the problem is our not understanding ourselves properly in the first place, and this is more akin to a psychological disorder than a physical one. But the distinction between the two related aspects of treatment holds good – don't do yourself unnecessary daily harm, keep working at improving what you are capable of. The precepts and skilfulness work together in this way. When we look at an ethical application of this we can see how.

As a father I may say I love my children. My underlying intentions toward them are all good; I wish to bring them up well and to do them no harm. In our everyday family life, I am often in a situation where I am concentrating on something other than them: doing a job around the house that has to be done; reading to relax; or writing a letter that should have been written yesterday. It occurs to my children that they have not had their pocket money, and they interrupt me to get it – they want it now! But right now I want to relax or get this job done. How much I love my children is not uppermost in my mind; my desires and theirs clash. I hold onto mine and they hold onto theirs; the result is anger and frustration, as I tell them to go away and come back later, while they tell me if I give it to them now they will not have to bother me again. It is a trivial example, but it is one of many that will recur during the day, and during every day that we are together.

As a Buddhist, how might I deal with this situation? What can I refer to? On one level the precepts, on another level the idea of skilfulness; on a third I can recognise the application of the Buddha's teaching on dukkha itself, and the Four Noble Truths. In the immediacy of the moment I cannot decide; I need to go away and think about it, but that is impractical and not what is required. I have to act, and how I act will depend upon what thoughts and feelings arise in my mind. I may try and apply the precepts, but I cannot do this mechanically; I have to be able to overcome my own desires to satisfy my children's. I also have to make a judgement about the way their request should be treated. But if my judgement is solely based on how I feel, it is likely to be awry. After the event, all these thoughts may go through my mind, but it is too late then, and so it will be the next time, and the time after, unless I address what is going on under the surface. In practice, showing my love to my children, though it is there, becomes a much more difficult intention to perform than I might imagine.

The practicality of Buddhist ethics

Looking at Buddhist ethics in this way affirms the importance of addressing a pervasive misconception that is often held about the relevance of ethics, and the relevance of Buddhist ideas to everyday life. Both can be separated from our daily activity and treated as intellectual mind-games, but this is not the intention. The purchase of both is their utility: do they make a difference to the way we live and the world we create? This question tests their efficacy and, at the same time, helps us penetrate what otherwise may seem baffling and remote concepts. For example, the significance of *anatta*, the doctrine of no-self, involves an awareness only gained by the practice of mindfulness. In turn, mindfulness makes us increasingly aware of the heedlessness of much of our thought and actions. In this way, Right

Speech, Action and Livelihood gain a practical significance that we can illustrate from reflection on our experience. Ignorance ceases to be a question of lack of theoretical knowledge; we can put our finger on exactly when it has determined the way we have behaved. Furthermore, we begin to realise that the view of ourselves that has prompted such actions (composed of desire and aversion) is the delusion that ensures this unsatisfactory state of affairs is maintained and replayed. I love my children, but I still behave to them in an inadequate and unskilful way. The goal of Buddhist ethics is to change this behaviour, to refine it, by increasing my capacity to create harmony and peacefulness in relations with myself and others. This is not just a matter of do's and don'ts, but rules do have their necessary place. It is not a matter of penetrating inscrutable concepts; but greater awareness involves more reflection. It is not a matter of retreating from the world, but of having a practice that prepares me for those situations in which it will be shown to be useful.

This analysis helps us to realise also that the Buddhist emphasis on intention is not about having the right sentiments or ignoring the effect of what we do. Buddhist morality is not a soft option based upon the wish to be a nice person or do good works. There is a rigour in Buddhist morality, because it conjoins both our intelligence, in the fullest sense of the term, and our feelings, in relation to what we will for ourselves and others, in progressing toward wisdom and compassion. This is why skilfulness plays such a central role, as the following Buddhist writer explains.

> According to Buddhist tradition there are two kinds of action, *kausalya* (Pali *kusala*) or skilful, and *akausalya* (Pali *akusala*) or unskilful. This is significant because the terms 'skilful' and 'unskilful', unlike the terms 'good' and 'bad', suggest that morality is very much a matter of intelligence. You cannot be skilful unless you can understand things, unless you can see possibilities and explore them. Hence morality, according to Buddhism, is as much a matter of intelligence and insight as one of good intentions and good feelings. After all, we have been told that the path to hell is paved with good intentions, but you could hardly say that the path to hell is paved with skilfulness. It just doesn't fit.
>
> (Sangharakshita, *A Guide to the Buddhist Path*,
> Windhorse Publications, 1990, p 140)

We can now see the moral sense of what appear at first to be simply abstract logical formulations, for example, the bare doctrinal formulation of cause and effect.

> That being thus this comes to be;
> from the coming to be of that, this arises;
> that being absent, this does not happen;
> from the cessation of that, this ceases.
> (*Majjhimanikāya II*, quoted in H. Saddhatissa, *Buddhist Ethics*,
> Wisdom Publications, 1987 p 28)

This can now be applied on both the grand scale (spelt out in the teaching on 'Dependent Origination', the theory of karma and the pictorial expression of the Buddhist world view in the Wheel of Becoming), and also in the minutiae of thought and action between one moment and the next. It is this second application that makes sense of things on a larger scale, and reveals ethics, the issue of how to live well or appropriately, to be the core of the Buddha's teaching. Nirvana may appear to be a wonderful dream – or a hideous annihilation – when viewed in a speculative fashion, but neither view is of any significance whatsoever. Chase Nirvana or run away from it; such thoughts, conceptions and actions are as erroneous as seeking a first cause or beginning. What matters is the here and now of separating delusion from understanding, and recognising the effect of doing so; what arises and what ceases, what is wholesome and what is not. This is at the heart of Buddhism and Buddhist ethics. It is the Dharma and the path to happiness, or what is also termed 'quietude of heart'.

Working on yourself and benefiting others

This may be introduced in the form of a story. My younger daughter has a habit, when being castigated for a mishap she has performed, such as breaking a cup or mislaying her recorder, with the refrain, 'I didn't mean to'. I believe her complaint is authentic; she is not just using it as an excuse, but really saying she doesn't believe she is truly at fault. However, as an adult, it is clear to me that 'not meaning to' does not solve the problem. Something more is required of her (and of me) if we are not to repeat the situation. I may reflect that the inadequacy lies in her thoughtlessness: if she were more aware of what was required of her, such things would happen less often! If she maintains the same stance in adulthood she will not receive a lot of sympathy. The point is this: whether you mean to do something or not relies upon being aware of what is required in being responsible for the cup or the recorder. When we take this into account, we cannot view doing the right things as just an impetuous activity – well-meaning but not well-considered, or as an unreflective wish to concentrate on that which we prefer to think about, in the moment, without regard to other things that also need to be considered. The answer to this problem lies in recognising responsibilities I may find more onerous, and in executing tasks in a way that requires more discipline than I would normally exercise. In other words, I have to work on *myself* in order to be of benefit to others. A well-meaning person with little regard to the effects of their action may be about as much use as a bull in a china shop! This applies whether we are talking about the home environment, aid sent to catastrophes occurring across the world, or diplomatic efforts to resolve crises.

'Working on yourself' in terms of awareness and discipline is of fundamental importance but, from a western point of view, coloured by our own cultural context, it can appear to have an individualistic emphasis, contrasting thinking of others with thinking of oneself. If this is also related to the traditional Buddhist communal form of monasticism, then is might appear as a retreat from social obligation; a form of self-obsession and introversion. But this is not the case. Self-development and the recognition of personal and social responsibility are inseparable. The principle holds good on the individual and the global scales; what matters is to keep the balance. In traditional Buddhist countries, the balance is kept by regarding monastic and lay life as interdependent aspects of the social order. In the West we have some difficulty with this, due to a very different social history. Nevertheless, it is important to consider what external environment, what pattern of daily life and what time spent in quietude to address issues, is necessary. This is one of the vital challenges to Buddhism today, as it spreads to the West and reconsiders its role in an increasingly westernised Asiatic world. For the westerner wishing to understand the Buddhist view, the important issue to consider may be how the Buddhist accent on self-development, or bhavana, can enrich the western emphasis (in real terms) on altruism. For Buddhists of course, at least in theory, the two are not distinct, since the one flows from and enriches the other, but that is not to say that Buddhists always get it right, or that social structures in one society necessarily serve the same ends in another. What must be confronted, however, is the naïve criticism that Buddhism falls short, morally speaking, where other traditions succeed. If anatta, mindfulness, skilfulness, wisdom and compassion are properly understood in relation to each other, there are no grounds for levelling such a criticism. Indeed, we might say that such scrutiny should be cast the other way.

The precepts and the dharmas

The precepts outline what to abstain from, and the dharmas are the qualities to cultivate. They go together, and it is important to recognise that whilst abstaining from the one negative state of mind resulting in negative action, the other, positive, state is encouraged. The precepts have already been mentioned in the first chapter. The basic dharmas, or ethical principles, are also five in number:

Abstaining from acts of harmfulness is an encouragement of metta, or loving kindness.
Abstaining from taking what is not given is an encouragement of *dana*, or generosity.
Abstaining from sexual misconduct is an encouragement of *santutthi*, or contentment.
Abstaining from false speech is an encouragement of *sacca*, or truthfulness.
Abstaining from intoxicants of the mind is an encouragement of *sati*, mindfulness or awareness.

Here, then, is the foundation of Buddhist practice (bhavana), the qualities without which no progress is possible. The precepts are held up as the fundamental code of Buddhist ethical life, not because they stop you doing what you might want, but because only to the extent that they are adhered to can the discipline required to progress be made possible.

Let us look at this discipline in more detail, this time using the fourth precept: abstention from false speech. As with all the others, false speech is rooted in craving, hatred or fear. False speech is a protective device which ignores truthfulness. The more you lie, the more acceptable the habit becomes, and the less important it is to be truthful. False speech goes further than direct lying, of course. Outright lies are its gross form, but it is also connected with many levels of communication. Right Speech, the fourth step of the Eightfold Path, is speech generated by affection and guided by discernment. It is to say something which is helpful in a given situation, and to a particular person or group of people. It is not the expression of anger, but equally it should not be talking for talk's own sake. It should be useful, and, by virtue of this, be meaningful also. Put bluntly, it means you should think carefully about what you are going to say and how you are going to say it. This requires self-restraint – another important quality for Buddhists. There is much that stands in the way of achieving this goal with all its implications, but perhaps the root of the matter is the need to develop honesty; not just the idea of being honest with others, but of being honest with oneself. Let us try an example.

I am in conversation with a friend, and we talk about what we have been doing during the week. My friend tells me that she applied for a job, went to the interview yesterday, and was told she had got it. Now she is wondering whether to accept it, but is obviously very excited at the prospect. She explains that, on the strength of this success, and because she will earn more money and have more status, she went out this morning and bought some new clothes. She wants to show me the clothes and tells me about all the new people she will meet, the places she will be travelling to, and the projects she will be in charge of.

When my friend knocked on my door this morning I was pleased to see her. Now I am no so sure. I want to feel pleased for her but I am finding it difficult. I want to say the right thing, but I lack the conviction to say it with any spontaneity. I have been doing mundane chores, and here is someone speaking of the excitement I would wish for my own life. Feelings arise that are difficult to suppress and, though my responses are conventionally appropriate to my role as friend, my heart is not in it.

We have all been in situations which give rise to such difficulties. But notice the levels on which Right Speech has to be addressed in order to be accomplished. Maybe the best I can do now is put on a good face, say the right things. But true affection and the capacity for sympathetic joy will require much more work in addressing the underlying reasons for my own dukkha which prevent me offering them to the world – or in this particular case, my friend. Restraint, discernment, awareness and acceptance all have to be available to me. Fundamentally, I must recognise that life will not present itself to me as I would wish it, and I must address and recognise my wishes for what they are – desire, aversion and fear – if I am to be able to communicate with real generosity. So the example of Right Speech also serves as an example for the other precepts. In this I must recognise that every action is as it is because of the thoughts that gave rise to it, and that progress on the Buddhist path is a matter of disciplined improvement, and of the cultivation of those qualities that will eventually make such situations no longer onerous, because the negative states that bring them about will have been replaced by positive ones. Ultimately we may even be able to replace our own dukkha with insight. As we listen, we discern the need of the other person and respond freely. Such a capacity to listen and respond is referred to as 'giving the gift of the Dharma', and this is a blessing to the world, freely given for its own sake and resulting in transformation.

We may view this progress from the one state to the other not in terms of a sudden transformation, but rather as the development of a skill. If I were learning to drive, swim or juggle, it would not be so different. I must recognise what I am getting right and getting wrong, and acknowledge what is improving as well as investigate what is not quite right. With all these things there are sudden breakthroughs. At first I am pretty useless; nothing goes right. Then a number of things come together, and something I once could not do at all is now possible. All of a sudden it seems effortless, and there is nothing in the way. That is how it is. When we think of this on a grand scale we can start to understand the Buddhist idea of the Bodhisattva, one who aspires to be a Buddha, and who acts for the weal of the world, to relieve its suffering.

Buddhism does not, of course, simply think in terms of individual ethics. A question which is often asked, especially by individuals who feel disempowered, is 'What can I do to change the whole situation?' Wars, famines and global catastrophes constantly confront us, in the news and in the media generally. Whilst we need to know about such events, we also have to feel able to respond to them, rather than retreat from them. In this respect the first precept is particularly significant. Most religious and ethical traditions make firm statements about not killing in a needless way, not murdering and abjuring senseless violence. But the first precept, abstention from harming living beings, is a commitment to non-violence. Whilst in theory this is a very noble aim, we would be mistaken to say it is not contentious.

We have so far illustrated situations in which we may wish to do the right thing but encounter difficulties in putting such a motivation into practice; this emphasises the importance of skilfulness in Buddhist ethics. We are often confronted by situations in which our ideals are overrun by a desire for revenge or a wish to inflict pain and retribution. Everyone may regret times when they acted impetuously and hurt someone else, perhaps physically but more often emotionally. Yet most of us recognise times when violence appears a necessary preventive measure in order to stop further suffering. Why should Buddhist teachings stand so resolutely against such a common-sense necessity? If I act out of a good motive, isn't my action thereby exonerated? In a Christian context, this is the point at which the Sermon on the Mount would be weighed alongside the Ten Commandments. The first is a much more radical teaching than the second, and the first precept aligns itself with this radical alternative.

So we start with the situation we find ourselves in, and accept that we are working on ourselves to influence the overall world that we live in, with the aspiration to be virtuous in all things. Ultimately this aspiration is to achieve harmlessness, but at present it is to be as kind as possible. On the one hand we may take this example from a Thai monk working in a particularly difficult area of Thailand, where there are pirates and fishermen who may be seen as rather rough and cruel people. We are told: 'Murder is quite common among them. So this monk just tries to encourage them not to kill each other. When these people come to the monastery he doesn't go round raising non-killing to the level of, "You shouldn't kill anything – not even a mosquito larva", because they couldn't accept that. Their livelihood depends very much on fishing and the killing of animals.' (Ven. Ajahn Sumedho, Cittaviveka: *Teachings from the Silent Mind*, Amaravati Publications, 1987, p 25) His teaching aims at gradually sensitising them in their everyday life to be less violent.

At the other extreme, we consider the situation of the Dalai Lama, exiled in this present life, from his country; many of his people are undergoing repression, and in some cases, torture. His response to such a dilemma tests the credulity of listeners across the world. He continues to eschew violence as a means to repatriation and freedom for his people, and his views can only be honoured on the basis of his personal integrity and stature. Whilst other calamities of a similar kind have evoked military reprisal and quests for violent intervention, the present incarnation of the Bodhisattva Avalokiteshvara (the embodiment of compassion) still affirms the need to seek peaceful ways of overcoming present injustice. The focus of the Buddhist view goes broader and deeper, more than just a response to immediate affairs. The *Dharma*, virtue, the precepts and the Eightfold Path cannot be affirmed if there is no practice of sila (Right Speech, Right Action and Right Livelihood) and, as a consequence, going for refuge may entail facing up to difficult responsibilities within a world driven by karmically negative forces.

Renunciation

No account of Buddhist morality would be complete without dwelling on the concept of renunciation, which is so central to the Buddhist view. It is apt to be misunderstood when it is seen as a curtailment of freedom and opportunity, but this is largely due to a reductionist understanding of such a rich concept. The important question is 'What does renunciation entail?'

Once the Buddha had set in motion the Wheel of the Law (Dharma) by preaching his first sermon, he spoke of having entered on the course that will make an end of suffering, and he stated that 'the road was declared by me when I had understood the removal of the darts'.

The darts (*salla*) are the hindrances or fetters that bind us to the round of rebirth. They symbolise lust, hatred, delusion, pride, false views, grief and indecision. When Buddhists speak about renunciation it is in relation to these things. Buddhist decisions about morality are necessarily undertaken with the knowledge that virtue itself lies in the renunciation of these things, and that whatever situation arises Right Action or Livelihood cannot be motivated by any of these forces. Whilst in humanitarian terms we may recognise fairness, or even retribution, as a way of dealing with the balance of events in life (on a personal or global scale), that course can never be the proper motivation of a Buddhist sensibility. Whatever takes place here and now is determined by the ongoing effect of karmic conditioning, and the eradication of this can only be initiated by the renunciant ideal. A short-term re-balancing of affairs, from a moral point of view, is not necessarily an improvement in the overall context of human history. We may witness this in the fact that the ending of one war or period of violence does not end violence altogether. The seeds of one conflict may be sown in the conclusion of a previous one. Necessarily, therefore, the ideal of renunciation has to take account of the continuous possibility of present suffering, whilst holding fast to the motivation that renunciation imposes. As with all ethical ideals found within the great religious traditions, the conflict between pragmatism and idealism is pronounced; but Buddhism, perhaps, identifies it more obviously than others, since renunciation brooks no compromise. Its strength lies in its overall vision but, understandably, this involves a commitment that is not easy to sustain.

Renunciation is intimately related to skilfulness, and thus to the notion of transforming the mind. There is an evolutionary sense to this interconnection, which is well expressed in the following passage by two Tibetan teachers:

> There are many ways of transforming the mind. The method presented here is intended to turn the mind from non-virtue to virtue. For instance, if we set about training our body, first we feel stiff and awkward. After performing physical exercises, however, our body becomes supple and agile and can adopt many postures which previously would have been difficult. It is evident that the body can gain a greater degree of flexibility by applying the appropriate exercises, and the same is true for the mind. Initially, we may have to endure many difficulties and hardships, but by making a concerted effort we can make our mind very supple. Endowed with this quality we may then engage in a great many skilful activities.

(Geshe Rabten and Geshe Dhargyey, *Advice from a Spiritual Friend*, Wisdom Publications, 1984, p 25)

Neither skilfulness nor virtue are gained from complacency. There is little to offer from such a safe haven that will benefit others. Helping people by saying things that renew them and allow them to face difficult situations, inevitably arises from sharing our own difficulties with them. We may not think we are speaking with wisdom, but rather voicing our own inadequacies; but the effect is more vitalising than platitudes of commiseration. Given that circumstance does not let us live exactly as we would wish according to our desires, this makes good sense, but we must often be pushed into realising it. This struggle is one that we must have with ourselves; but it is a creative one, the benefits of which become tangible in practice. The Buddhist scriptures offer advice as to how to accomplish it. Here are some verses related to transforming anger. The purpose of recollecting such advice is to remove the obstacles to generating metta (loving kindness).

Admonition to Oneself

The fourth method: if, however, in spite of one's efforts, irritation continues to arise, one should think thus:

Suppose an enemy has hurt you
In what is now his domain,
Why try yourself as well to hurt
Your mind? That is not his domain.

This anger that you entertain
Is gnawing at the very roots
Of all the virtues that you guard –
Where is there such a fool as you!

Another does ignoble deeds,
So you are angry – how is this?
Do you then want to copy, too,
The sort of acts that he commits?

Suppose another, to annoy,
Provokes you with some odious act,
Why suffer anger to spring up,
And do as he would have you do?

If you get angry, then may be
You make him suffer, may be not;
Though with the hurt that anger brings
You certainly are punished now.

If anger-blinded enemies
Set out to tread the path of woe,
Do you, by getting angry too,
Intend to follow heel to toe?

If hurt is done you by a foe
Because of anger on your part,
Then put your anger down, for why
Should you be harassed needlessly?

Since states last but a moment's time,
Those aggregates, by which was done
The odious act, have ceased, so now
What is it you are angry with?

Whom shall he hurt, who seeks to hurt
Another, in the other's absence?
Your presence is the cause of hurt;
Why are you angry, then, with him?

(*Visuddhimagga 308*, copyright H. Saddhatissa. Reprinted from
Buddhist Ethics with permission of Wisdom Publications,
361 Newbury Street, Boston, Massachusetts, USA.)

7

— MORAL ISSUES —

For Buddhists, all moral issues are approached with the following in mind.

- Purifying the Mind and Developing Wisdom.
- Following the Precepts.
- The Law of Karma and Rebirth.
- Intentionality and Skilfulness.
- Developing Loving Kindness and Compassion.

These are not separate considerations but rather the factors which ensure that what one does is a blessing to the world, rather than a corruption of it. Sila (ethical action) is the expression of dharma (truth); carried out in the course of everyday life and moral decision-making, it frees the world from dis-ease and confusion.

However, for Buddhists, there is no overall authority that legislates right and wrong on particular issues. There is guidance, and there are limits, but the task of making difficult decisions, within the framework of the precepts, is the individual's responsibility. The following issues have been chosen to illustrate this, and to represent particular focuses of Buddhist concern.

The natural world

Animal welfare

Rebirth, when aligned to the doctrine of harmlessness, leads Buddhists to emphasise compassionate attitudes to all living things.

The *Culla-Vagga*, verse 6, states that:

> Creatures without feet have my love,
> And likewise those that have two feet,
> And those that have four feet I love,
> And those, too, that have many feet.

> May those without feet harm me not,
> And those with two feet cause no hurt,
> May those with four feet harm me not,
> Nor those who many feet possess.

> Let creatures, all, all things that live,
> All beings of whatever kind,
> See nothing that will bode them ill!
> May naught of evil come to them!

The *Buddhist Declaration on Nature* affirms:

> The fact that (animals) may be incapable of communicating their feelings is no more an indication of apathy or insensibility to suffering or happiness than in the case of a person whose faculty of speech is impaired . . . .

> There is a striking similarity between exterminating the life of a wild animal for fun and terminating the life of an innocent human being at the whim of a more capable and powerful person . . . . [Buddhism is a] system which propagates the theory of rebirth and life after death, it maintains that in the continuous birth and rebirth of sentient beings (not only on this planet but in the universe as a whole) each being is related to us ourselves, just as our own parents are related to us in this life . . . .

> We regard our survival as an undeniable right. As co-inhabitants of this planet, other species too have this right for survival. And since human beings as well as other non-human sentient beings depend upon the environment as the ultimate source of life and well-being, let us share the conviction that the conservation of the environment, the restoration of the imbalance caused by our negligence in the past, be implemented with courage and determination.

> (*Buddhist Declaration on Nature*, Assisi, 29 September 1986)

The *Sutta Nipata* echoes these sentiments:

> May creatures all abound
> in weal and peace; may all

be blessed with peace always;
all creatures
weak or strong,
all creatures great and small;
creatures unseen or seen,
dwelling afar or near,
born or awaiting birth,
– may all be blessed with peace!

Just as with her own life
a mother shields from hurt
her own, her only, child, –
let all embracing thoughts
for all that lives be thine,
– an all-embracing love
for all the universe
in all its heights and depths
and breadth, unstinted love,
unmarred by hate within,
not rousing enmity.

Ecology

The Buddhist emphasis on harmony and ecological balance is extended to the whole of the natural world. Buddhists see a need to ensure the balance of nature as an ethical priority. In the *Buddhist Declaration on Nature* at the Conference of World Faiths in Assisi they stated:

> Hence Buddhism is a religion of love, understanding and compassion, and committed towards the ideal of non-violence. As such, it also attaches great importance to wildlife and the protection of the environment on which every being in this world depends for survival.

In the West, where ecological issues have gained some prominence, Buddhist initiatives have also been in evidence. For example, in 1979, The English Sangha Trust bought an area of West Sussex woodland for a Forest Retreat Sangha. This is now the focus of a conservation project based on the Buddhist idea of harmony with all forms of life. The wood is being restored to its original character having previously been exploited commercially, by the implementation of a monocultural system of agriculture, wherein are planted trees of a species suitable for growing as a cash crop. The wood is now seen as a place of peace and tranquillity, where monks and nuns can engage in solitary meditation and retreat, and where indigenous wildlife can flourish.

In 1991 the Samye Ling Tibetan Centre in Scotland launched the 'Holy Island Project'. This has resulted in buying Holy Isle, just off the Isle of Arran, to use as a place of spiritual retreat and as a nature reserve. Four hundred years ago, the island was the site of a monastery, and the project intends to restore it to its former use, but as an interdenominational retreat centre as well as a facility specifically for Buddhist practitioners.

Vegetarianism

Given the first precept, it might seem logical that all Buddhists are vegetarian; however, this is not always the case, as this comment demonstrates:

> 'Is it permissible to eat meat?' I asked a learned and holy Tibetan lama. 'Certainly, although if you are practising meditation on compassion it could be counterproductive.'
>
> 'Is it not the case that the one who eats meat bears responsibility for the killing?' The holy man looked astonished. Patiently he explained to me basic Buddhist truths which I should have mastered lives ago. Of course not. The one who eats meat a) intends to eat, and b) may or may not intend to eat meat. Meat is, as a matter of fact, what is being eaten. But nowhere in the mental states of our reverend gourmand is there an intention to kill. In fact, in the Tibetan tradition, by the monk reciting suitable formulae over the juicy curry, the goat may actually obtain a more favourable rebirth than would otherwise be the case. Thus, even while eating meat, our monk can generate compassion and do good towards a creature which was already dead, and dead through no wish of the monk himself.'
>
> (Paul Williams in C. Erricker (ed), *Teaching World Religions*, Heinemann, 1993, p 46)

Nevertheless, in the West especially, some Buddhists do make out a strong case for encouraging the vegetarian viewpoint.

In *A Buddhist Case for Vegetarianism*, Roshi Philip Kapleau cites his own students often asking the question, 'Does Buddhism prohibit meat-eating?' He includes a letter illustrating the dilemma that many westerners face when trying to convert Buddhist principles into practice, which runs thus:

> We were drawn to Buddhism by its teaching of respect for all forms of life, human as well as non-human. But being new to it, we are confused and concerned about one thing. To practise Buddhism correctly, is it necessary to give up eating meat? There seems to be no agreement among Buddhists on this point. We've heard that in Japan and Southeast Asia lay Buddhists and even monks and priests eat meat, and that teachers in the United States and other Western countries do the same. But here in Rochester we're told that you and your students are vegetarians. Do the Buddhist scriptures forbid the eating of meat? If so, for what reasons? If they don't forbid it, why, may we ask, are you a vegetarian? We would become vegetarians ourselves if we were sure that by doing so we could become more deeply involved in Buddhism. But if that were not the case, we'd rather not give up meat, partly because all our friends eat it. Also, we do have some reservations from a health standpoint about a vegetarian diet.
>
> (Roshi Philip Kapleau, *A Buddhist Case for Vegetarianism*,
> Rider, 1983, p 4)

Underlying this concern is the idea that meat gives strength and energy, and contributes to a balanced diet. Kapleau cites the American philosopher, Thoreau, in answer to such a question:

> When asked by a farmer 'I hear you don't eat meat. Where do you get your strength (read 'protein')?' Thoreau, pointing to the husky team of horses drawing the farmer's wagon, replied, 'Where do they get their strength?' Kapleau further contends that according to modern medical opinion, the issue is now beyond speculation. Vegetarians, it seems are on the side of the angels.
>
> (ibid., pp 4–5)

He goes on to cite the pain and suffering involved in animal slaughter, and in the way in which animals are reared and transported in environments solely conditioned by economic greed. Vegetarians would maintain that meat-eating represents a tacit acceptance of human greed, and a complicity in its process. So, one may ask, should

Buddhists not therefore align themselves with the principle of vegetarianism? The issue can be extended further, as this sentiment from an ancient Chinese verse indicates, linking animal slaughter to bad karma:

> For hundreds of thousands of years
> the stew in the pot
> has brewed hatred and resentment
> that is difficult to stop.
> If you wish to know why there are disasters
> of armies and weapons in the world,
> listen to the piteous cries
> from the slaughterhouse at midnight.

(ibid., p 17)

Of course, the principle of rebirth also plays a part in this argument. In Mahayana Buddhism, one of the themes for contemplation is that, in the endless cycle of rebirths, not a single being has not been our mother, father, husband or other relative in some way. This breaks down the species division between humans and non-humans, and does not allow us to think of other creatures as separate, inferior life forms. All life therefore becomes sacred.

Nevertheless, traditionally, Buddhism is not exclusively vegetarian. One contemporary Buddhist, of the Tibetan tradition, in answer to the question, 'Can monks eat meat?' replies,

> Strictly speaking, from the point of view of the *vinaya*, a monk should not eat meat. However, most Tibetan monks do eat meat and I have been influenced by them so I eat it too. Originally, when I was first ordained and living in a monastery in Nepal most of my time was spent in study and meditation so I didn't eat meat. We tended to get up early and go to bed early and a vegetarian diet made sleep lighter and the mind clearer for meditation. But when I started travelling and leading a more 'normal' lifestyle – working – I just found that I was too hungry at night and did not feel so strong. So I started eating meat.

(P. Connolly and C. Erricker, *The Presence & Practice of Buddhism*, West Sussex Institute of Higher Education, 1985, p 111)

So the answer to the question 'Are Buddhists vegetarian?' is this: some are and some are not. However, western Buddhists are certainly sensitive to this issue, and many see a sensitising of our way of life as a commitment to vegetarianism.

There is a caveat to this, however. Monks, as mendicants, when presented with *dana* (their meal of the day, put into their alms-bowl by lay Buddhists), are expected to accept such generosity unquestioningly. Traditionally, giving meat is often seen by lay Buddhists as a generous gesture, and it would not be appropriate for the monks to refuse.

Human society

Capital punishment and imprisonment

In principle, and following the first precept, Buddhism deplores the taking of life under any circumstances. However, in some Buddhist countries, notably Thailand and Burma, the death penalty is exercised in certain cases. One of the most important teachers in Buddhist history, Buddhaghosa, considered the act of killing and murder as follows:

> 'Taking life' means to kill anything that lives. The precept says that you should not strike or kill any living being. 'Anything that lives' is anything that has what is called the 'life-force'. This includes all members of the animal kingdoms as well as humans. 'Taking life' means killing or trying to kill deliberately, by word or action.
>
> With regard to animals, it is worse to kill large ones than small ones. This is because you have to make a much greater effort to kill large ones. Even where the effort is the same, the difference in importance has to be taken into account. When it comes to human beings, the killing is considered to be worse if the person killed was a good (virtuous) person. Apart from that, the seriousness of the offence is also measured by how much the murderer wanted the killing to happen.
>
> (quoted in J.Rankin et al, *Religion and Ethics*, Longman, 1991, p 152)

Whilst the act of killing is effectively prohibited in principle, the important issue is to be compassionate in any circumstance. Given this, one should offer this compassion to anyone, whatever their circumstance and whatever acts they may have committed.

One Buddhist mission which promotes this principle is a chaplaincy service for prisoners in the United Kingdom. The purpose of this venture is to bring some serenity, contemplation and desire for altruistic action into prisoners' lives. 'Buddha groves' (areas for contemplation in which Buddha images have been placed) have been established in some British prisons. The director of the British Prison Chaplaincy Service explains:

> My purpose in encouraging the placing of these simple Buddhist shrines in the prisons is twofold and has nothing to do with proselytising or trying to win converts to Buddhism. The Prison Service admits that prisoners should be allowed to practise their religion and that places of worship should be provided for the prisoners of all religious faiths. Our first objective then, in a very modest way, is to help meet that standard by providing the few Buddhist prisoners with a focus for their devotion and meditation practice. And, secondly, for those who are not Buddhist we hope that having the opportunity to rest their eyes on something as serene and peaceful as a Buddha-Rupa will help them quieten their minds and bestow a little respite from the turmoil so often about and within them.

The particular results of their efforts are exemplified thus:

> Inmates in Risley (prison) fasted recently so that the money that would have been used to feed them could be diverted to the starving in Rwanda.
>
> (Ajahn Khammadhammo, *The Forest Hermitage Newsletter*,
> September 1994)

Abortion and mercy killing

In this area, the Five Precepts once more prevail as guiding principles – especially the first, which is linked with the quality of compassion. However, given that there is no overriding authority in ethical matters in Buddhism, each individual must make his or her own decision about the circumstances in which they find themselves.

Abortion, in principle, is to be avoided, though, as the following comment shows, it is not absolutely forbidden.

> Although abortion appears to, perhaps really does, abrogate the first principle, it might on balance, and in particular circumstances, yet be considered a necessity for compassionate reasons.
>
> (General Secretary, The Buddhist Society)

However, groups motivated by the Buddhist principle of compassion do tend to attach a particular significance to birth – despite it not being linked to a doctrine of creation – as is demonstrated here with regard to doctors and midwives.

> Every birth is Holy. I think that a midwife must be religious, because the energy she is dealing with is Holy. She needs to know that other people's energy is sacred.
>
> (Ina May Gaskin, *Spiritual Midwifery*,
> The Book Publishing Co., 1980, p 282)

War

It hardly needs stating that every world religion is, in principle, against violence. But, in practice, the question of course remains as to what to do when violent action is required to preserve a particular faith or culture.

When a British mission, led by Younghusband, sought to enter Tibet by force at the beginning of the twentieth century, the Tibetans put down their arms and retreated from their borders. This might be seen as an act of cowardice, but the Buddhist motivation was to reduce the amount of harm incurred by conflict. The message of the Dalai Lama, in exile today, echoes this action. Politically naïve as it may appear, Buddhists have generally taken this stance of non-resistance in most violent situations (although armed resistance to the Chinese has been organised by some Tibetans within Tibet, with the involvement of the CIA).

Scripture and tradition both point to social harmony being the result of inner peace. The *Dhammapada* states:

> Though one man conquer a thousand times a thousand men in battle, he who conquers himself is the greatest warrior . . .
>
> Better than sovereignty over the earth, better than the heaven-state, better than dominion over all the worlds is the first step on the noble path . . .

And,

> Hatred does not cease by hatred, hatred ceases only by love. This is the eternal law.

Of course, the ideal is not always matched by the actuality, as the problems faced by Tamils in Sri Lanka in recent years have demonstrated!

Suicide

Suicide is not a moral fault, properly speaking, because morality is directly concerned with what we do to others. The great Buddhist teacher Nagarjuna explained:

> According to the *Treatise on Discipline*, suicide is not murder. Fault and merit result respectively from a wrong done to others or the good done to others. It is not by caring for one's own body or killing one's own body that one acquires merit or commits a misdeed.
>
> (*Buddhist Studies Review*, Vol 4, no 2 1987, p 106)

However, if one person incites another to suicide, that is a different matter:

> If a monk, with deliberate intent, takes with his own hands the life of a human being . . . if he himself gives him a weapon and tells him to kill himself; if he praises death to him; if for example he says to him, 'Fie on you! What good does this miserable life do you? Far better to die than live', in such a way that the other conceives in his heart a delight in dying; if in these various fashions he tells him to die or praises death to him, and later that man, because of this, dies, that monk is blameworthy of a very grave offence and should be excluded from the Community . . .
>
> (ibid., p 105)

Suicide is, however – like all conscious or voluntary acts – subject to the law of Karma. Suicide is folly, insofar as taking one's own life is the outcome of the desire to annihilate oneself; for the fruit of that act is a rebirth in the samsaric realm, and hence further suffering.

Nevertheless, suicide is justified in the case of the 'Noble Ones', who have already cut off desire. There can be no possible further fruition to their actions. Death is a way of severing their last link with this world and passing into Nirvana, since they have done what had to be done. A test case is that of Valkali: Valkali was a disciple of the Buddha who became sick and experienced great suffering. The Buddha was told of this, and came to where Valkali lay.

> The Master approached and said to him: 'Do not move, Valkali, there are seats quite near and I shall sit there.'
>
> Having sat down, he went on: 'Friend, is it tolerable? Is it

viable? Are the painful feelings you are experiencing on the decrease and not on the increase?'

'No, Master,' replied Valkali, 'it is neither tolerable nor viable. The painful feelings are on the increase and not on the decrease.'

'Then have you some regret and some remorse?'

'Yes, Master,' confessed Valkali, 'I have much regret and much remorse.'

'Does your conscience reproach you for something from the moral point of view?'

'No, my conscience does not reproach me for anything from the moral point of view.'

'And yet,' stated the Buddha, 'you have regret and remorse.'

'This is because for a long time I have wanted to go and look at the Master, but I do not find the strength in my body to do it.'

'For shame, Valkali!' cried the Buddha, 'What good would it do you to see my body of filth? Valkali, whoever sees my Doctrine, sees me; whoever sees me sees my Doctrine.'

Having spoken thus, the Buddha went to the Vulture Peak, while Valkali had himself carried to the Black Rock on the Seers' Mount. During the night two deities warned the Buddha that Valkali was thinking of liberating himself and that, once liberated, he would be delivered.

The Buddha dispatched some monks to Valkali to tell him:

'Blameless will be your death, blameless the end of your days.'

'Return to the Master,' said Valkali, 'and in my name prostrate yourselves at his feet. Be sure and tell him that I no longer feel any doubt regarding the transitory, painful and unstable nature of all the phenomena of existence.'

The monks had hardly left when Valkali 'took the knife' and killed himself. The Buddha, being doubtful about this, immediately went to the Black Rock in the company of several disciples. Valkali lay dying on his couch, his shoulders turned to the right, for it is thus that the Noble Ones die. A cloud of black dust moved around him.

'Do you see, O Monks,' the Buddha asked, 'that cloud of dust which is drifting in all directions around the corpse? It is Mara, the Malign One who is seeking the whereabouts of Valkali's consciousness. But Valkali's consciousness is nowhere: Valkali is in complete Nirvana.'

Hence the Noble Ones who have triumphed over delusion and eliminated passion can, once their task is done, speed the hour of deliverance by voluntarily taking their own lives. Whatever the means used, act of will, recourse to the supernormal, or quite simply the rope or knife, their suicide is 'blameless'.

(ibid., pp 110–111)

Altruistic sacrifice

Equally, Bodhisattvas who gave their life altruistically for other beings were regarded as noble and blameless; one such was the Bodhisattva Vessantara, whose action towards the hungry tigress in the *Vessantara Jataka* is recorded in Chapter 4.

Auto-cremation

There is another form of religious suicide, known as auto-cremation. The burning of their own bodies by Buddhist monks in Vietnam, as a protest against the regime, arguably falls into this category. The important point in these events is, of course, not the act itself, but the question of its motive or intention, and the state of mind in which it was carried out.

Gender and equality

In all the major religious traditions of the world this is a vexed issue, largely for historical and social reasons. In the times of those who founded traditions the status of women tended to be subservient to men. In Indian culture, the caste system provided a rigorous definition of woman's role. For example, the question of a dowry, to be paid by the wife's parents to those of the husband, was also an indication of what was expected of her in the future.

In Buddhism the caste system was abolished, even though the monastic nature of the movement made the Buddha reticent to receive women into the order. The segregation of males and females was strictly observed in the context of renunciation, which emphasised the importance of avoiding situations that could inflame lustful desires.

However, women were accepted in both lay and monastic environments. The role of the mother, as one who gave and who was worthy of compassion, was stressed. The notion of rebirth actually accentuated the recognition that gender difference was not a fundamental determinant of identity. As the tradition evolved, so women played their part. When Buddhism extended beyond India to Sri Lanka, an order of nuns was requested for the island. Nevertheless, conservative social influences have tended to ensure that, on the whole, the role of women in traditionally Buddhist countries today is not equal to that of men, whether in the monastic Sangha or lay life. In the Theravadin tradition there is some difficulty regarding the status of nuns, since full ordination died out in the lineage over the course of time, and western female Buddhists who decide to take up the monastic life are duly prevented from achieving fully ordained status. Therefore they are, at present, subservient in status to any ordained monk, regardless of the number of years they have been in the Sangha. This is an issue that the western branches of Theravada Buddhism are constantly seeking to address.

In other branches of Buddhism the issue has evolved differently. A woman is spiritual head of the reformed Soto-Zen Church, as Abbess of Shasta Abbey in California, and Throssel Hole Priory in the United Kingdom. The Reverend Jiyu-Kennett was certified as Dharma Heir and fully licensed teacher by her master, the Very Reverend Keido Chisan Koho, Zenji.

In Tibetan Buddhism there have always been female Boddhisattvas, who have been the subject of devotion. Green and White Tara, embodying compassion, are the most obvious examples. Kuan Ying (the female form of Chenrezig or Avalokiteshvara, in Chinese and Japanese Buddhism) is also venerated. However, as often tends to be the case, this esteem is not wholly transferred to the status of women in these societies! As far as equality is concerned, there is still a way to go, but western Buddhism could provide the lead in this respect, because it is such a significant issue in western society. The FWBO acknowledges, with some qualification, the value of the feminist movement.

> Feminism . . . could be described as a movement that demands – or insists – that women should have access to all the facilities they require for their development as human beings; it asserts that they should not be confined or limited to any particular range of facilities or activities; and it encourages them to take more initiative, be more independent, and to function as

individuals in their own right, rather than being mere extensions or supports to the men in their lives. Feminism of this sort is quite compatible with Buddhism and the spiritual life . . . .

At the hub of the FWBO we therefore find a unified Order of women and men; everything in the Order is open to women and men; they take the same ordination and vows; they exercise the same functions at public centres; they practise the same meditations, study the same texts, and so on. In the FWBO we feel that no one should be excluded from the process of higher human development, whether on the grounds of sex, race, colour, level of education, or social position.

(*Golden Drum*, Windhorse Publications, No 7,
November–January 1987/8 p 13)

8

THE
— SOCIAL ORDER —

Ordination

Ordination generally entails taking up the mendicant life and 'going forth' as a monk or nun. In the Theravada tradition this is known as *bhikku ordination*, and follows on from the procedure first established by the Buddha when he ordained his first disciples, saying *'ehi bhikkhu!'* ('come bhikkhu!') after his first sermon in the Deer Park at Sarnath.

Candidates for ordination will already be *anagarikas* (novices). The ceremony will take place within a *sima* (a specially-defined area). An *Upajjhaya* (Preceptor) must officiate. He will be a senior monk, head of an order or senior incumbent of a monastery, invested with this responsibility. The candidates must be able to recite the *Patimokkha* (rules of discipline). Before the ceremony, new robes will have been made for the candidates, dyed brown or saffron. After it, they will be bound by the 227 rules of the monastic community and the Ten Precepts. In the Mahayana tradition the conventions and ceremonies vary, but the commitment is essentially the same. The robes worn are black in the Zen tradition and maroon in the Tibetan.

Celibacy

The *Vinaya* (Code of Discipline) orders monastic life, which demands celibacy. It is worth noting, however, that in certain Japanese, Korean and Tibetan Orders it is possible for monks and nuns to marry, though this is the exception rather than the rule. The Western Buddhist Order does not, strictly speaking, have monks and nuns.

They may be married with families or be single. However, celibacy is practised by some Order members. Those with families may still choose to live in single-sex communities, as this comment by a Western Buddhist Order member illustrates:

> Some people are surprised that I have a child and that I am an Order member who has gone for refuge to the Buddha and Sangha. Chastity, living in a community of men, and having a child, with the mother living in a women's community with the child, is cooperatively worked out. All Order members are working towards happy celibacy, contentment. That is certainly what I'm working toward. The primary thing is that I remain clear about being a Buddhist first and a parent second, for the sake of myself and the child. If I lose sight of that I'm lost really. What children need is clear positive emotion from the adults around them. I need the conditions to support positivity and clarity.
>
> (FWBO member)

Weddings and marriage

Marriage is regarded in Buddhism as a social and civil matter. Monks therefore do not officiate at weddings, nor are they allowed to be present at the ceremony. Monks will bless a marriage as a separate event, after the ceremony, but the distinction between this and the ceremony itself is quite clear. As one Theravada Buddhist puts it:

> It's not according to the *Vinaya*, which is the code of conduct for the monks. They are excluded from taking part in these ceremonies, because the Buddhist monk is a person who has renounced worldly life. He is working on his own salvation, and he is in a monastery which has been provided.
>
> (John Bowker, *Worlds of Faith*, BBC, 1983, p 207)

Family life

Since Buddhism is traditionally centred upon monastic life and the quest for liberation, it might seem that Buddhists would have little to say about married life and bringing up children. However, more than ninety-five per cent of Buddhists are lay people, with these issues very much at the centre of their lives.

Sangha has a larger meaning than just 'monastic community',

indeed, had the Buddha not spread his message to lay people the tradition would not have developed in the way that it has. The importance of the interdependent relationship between monastic and lay society was always emphasised by the Buddha, and with good reason, since, given the doctrine of rebirth, our station changes in successive lives and the merit accrued by good karma in one life is the only means to elevation in the next. Thus the significance of how one lives life as a lay person, and the way in which children are nurtured are important issues in Buddhist society which have led to the observance of specific rules and customs.

The Buddha said: 'A wise man should avoid unchastity as if it were a pit of burning cinders. One who is not able to live in a state of celibacy should at least not break the purity of another man's wife.' (*Suttanipata*, v.396)

The importance of the family

In the Buddha's Discourses there is much advice to householders on the importance of family life and how it should be conducted. The *Rukkhadamma Jataka* compares the strength of family life to the trees of the forest, which are able to withstand the force of the wind, when a solitary tree, however large, cannot.
(*Jataka*, Vol, 1, v. 329.)

The metaphor is apt for the significance of both family life and Sangha generally, suggesting that family ties and spiritual friendship encourage growth in the Dharma and resistance to samsaric conditions. The *Sigalovada Suttanta* gives the most specific advice on lay society and family life. Sigola was a young man who showed no interest in the Dharma, but who was entreated by his dying father to worship the six quarters of the earth and sky. Ignorant of the meaning of this, he was met one morning by the Buddha taking this advice literally, worshipping in every direction. The Buddha explained the six quarters to him as parents, teachers, wife and children, friends and associates, employees, religious teachers and priests. In each of these relationships certain duties pertain.

Parents and children

In the relationship between parent and child, the child should:

- support his or her parents;

- perform their duties for them;
- keep up the family and family traditions;
- be worthy of his or her heritage;
- offer alms in honour of departed relatives.

The parent should:

- restrain the children from evil;
- direct them toward the good;
- attend to their education;
- see them married at a proper age;
- hand over their inheritance.

(*Digha-Nikaya* lll,180, quoted in H. Saddhatissa, *Buddhist Ethics*, Wisdom Publications, 1987, p 118)

This description of duties can be complimented by a story illustrating the spirit of the relationship between parents and children that Buddhism seeks to develop:

Red Beans and Rice

There was once a director of a big company in Japan. He was elected president of a special club for businessmen. At the fancy dinner party to celebrate his election he served all his guests a dish of red beans and rice. In Japan, this dish is served when you want to wish someone well-being in the future. But at this grand dinner, this dish seemed out of place. The director was moved to explain why he had served the dish. He told everyone that it commemorated an incident in his life.

He was born and lived in a very poor farming family. His family was so poor that he grew to realise that however hard he might work on the land, he would never be able to produce enough from it to be able to care for his parents in their old age or to try to help educate his brothers and sisters. He decided that he would have to go to a town to find some other work. However, he was very aware that in Japan for an elder son to leave the land and his family was a source of great sadness. After much thought he resolved to make his departure at night, secretly. So he packed a small bundle for travel.

Long before dawn he made ready to leave his home. He was

just about to slip out of the kitchen door when he saw that his mother, who was normally asleep at that time, instead was up and working in the kitchen. Without turning to look at him she spoke.

'I've prepared some red beans and rice for you. Eat it before you go.'

He sat down in front of it at the small kitchen table. His mother brought over some hot soup as well. He was so close to tears that he could not eat anything. Seeing this his mother said, 'Maybe since you've just got up you may not be hungry. I'll take the rice from your bowl and make it into rice balls which you can carry with you and eat later.

He received the rice balls from her and left the house into the dark of the night. Following the dark road to the station, he cried all of the way. He went off to the town and worked very hard. Even though he made a fortune, he could never forget that dish of red beans and rice. If he thought about doing something bad, the memory of the red beans and rice stopped him.

At the dinner party, the businessman said, 'There are many people here who are much finer than I am, but in spite of that I have been elected as president. What gave me this honour is red beans and rice. Therefore I would like you also to eat it.'

When an old Zen teacher heard this story he was very moved. Not only by the maternal love that was demonstrated, but by the superb wisdom of the mother shown by her willingness to let him go. Somehow, she knew exactly what her son was thinking and what it was that he had to do.

(Ven. Morinaga Soko Roshi, *Rainbows Magazine*, Amaravati Publications, July 1994, p 4)

Husband and wife

In the relationship between husband and wife, the husband should:

- be courteous to his wife;
- respect her;
- be faithful;
- hand over authority to her;
- provide her with clothes and adornments.

The wife should:

- perform her household duties well;
- be hospitable to relatives;
- be faithful;
- protect the family income;
- be skilled and industrious in her duties.

> (*Digha Nikaya*, Vol, III, 190, quoted in H. Saddhatissa,
> *Buddhist Ethics*, Wisdom Publications, 1987, p 120)

Spiritual friendship

The idea of spiritual friendship underpins relationships within Buddhist community life, and is of particular importance in the bond between husband and wife.

> If the matter of selection of the family into which one is born in the present existence is closely connected with the karmic effects of previous lives, the selection of one's friends is clearly more directly associated with the circumstances and acts of the current life. Physiologically, the world is perpetuated by the family relationship, but the Buddha has also given the quality of making friends as one which is instrumental in 'making the world go round'. The person who is kindly, who makes friends, makes welcome, is free from avarice, is understanding, is a conciliator, such a one obtains good repute. Generosity, kindly speech, doing good to whatever person, fairness in all things, everywhere as is fit and proper, these are indeed the means on which the world turns, just as a chariot moves on quickly depending on the pin of a wheel axle.
>
> (*Digha Nikaya* III, 192 quoted in H. Saddhatissa, *Buddhist Ethics*, Wisdom Publications, 1987.)

The *Sanyutta Nikaya* says:

> It is not easy to find a being who has not been your mother, or your father, your brother, your sister or your son or daughter . . .
>
> (*Sanyutta Nikaya*, II, 189)

From this we can see that all relationships are meant to be approached in the same way, and with the same virtues and conduct in mind. Spiritual friendship is the key to this, whether for monk or for lay person, but in considering the relationship between husband and wife this is the essential quality – the pin that turns the wheel of family life. As one Buddhist, a member of the Friends of the Western Buddhist Order, explains:

> Perhaps the most radical changes in our attitudes to marriage occur when we begin to develop spiritual friendships, for here we discover the delights, the joys, of a truly human relationship in which there is no longer the aspect of two insecure people trying to prop each other up. Instead we find ourselves striving toward the same sublime ideal as our friend. We can face up to difficulties in our friendships by trying to bring more and more of our ideals into our communication with each other. We urge each other on to become more independent, to let our qualities shine out, to overcome weaknesses.
>
> (*Golden Drum*, Windhorse Publications, Number 7, p 7)

Birth and upbringing

Traditionally, before her baby's birth, a mother-to-be may visit a temple to receive blessings from the monks. Soon after the birth, too, babies are taken to the temple to receive blessings. Many Buddhists give their children names which begin with auspicious sounds, and a monk may be consulted as to suitable names. Some western families may wish to give Asian names to their children. Later on in their lives, boys in Burma and Thailand may take temporary ordination as part of their education. This will last for only a matter of weeks in most cases. This rite of passage is unavailable at present to Buddhists in western countries. Some efforts are being made, however, to establish a ceremony marking children's commitment to a Buddhist way of life:

Coming of Age: A Buddhist Way

On March 12th, I celebrated my 13th birthday at the Devon Vihara. I decided to do this because my cousin and my friend are both having a Barmitzvah this year. (A Barmitzvah is a Jewish ceremony celebrating coming of age.) I decided that I wanted to find a Buddhist way to celebrate my 13th birthday and the beginning of my adult years. So I talked with Ajahn Santacitto at the Devon Vihara and he liked the idea very much.

The day before the event I stayed at the Vihara and helped with various jobs. I was also preparing myself for the day ahead.

I wore white clothing which represents purity and was trying to keep the precepts. For the celebration itself, I invited lots of people to come along.

The day started with the offering of a dana meal to the monks, followed by Paritta chanting, precepts and a short Dhamma talk by Ajahn Santacitto. All of these I requested in Pali by myself. After the chanting and the Dhamma talk, other people offered reflections on what it is to be a man. The ceremony ended by planting a Douglas Fir tree outside. It came from our front garden so it felt like part of our family was left at the Vihara. It was nice to plant something living that would grow big and strong. It felt symbolic of the day and we could see it year after year and remember the occasion.

Lots of people gave me nice presents including the monks at the Devon Vihara who gave me a Buddha rupa.

I enjoyed the whole day and thought it went really well. I especially enjoyed staying at the Vihara by myself beforehand.

(*Rainbows Magazine*, Amaravati Publications, July 1994, p 5)

Religious observance

Observing Buddhist families keep a Buddha statue in the home, prominently positioned and well above the ground. This acts as a shrine; in some family homes there may be a separate shrine room. As in the monastery or temple, pujas or short services will be conducted here daily, and especially on full moon or festival days. Offerings of flowers, candles and incense are given and the precepts and refuges taken. Food is placed in front of the Buddha as a sign of generosity.

Families may also attend the local monastery or temple on observance days, when they will take the traditional offerings (dana, or food for the monks and nuns in the Theravadin tradition), and reaffirm their commitment by taking the refuges and precepts. This may be followed by meditation and chanting.

Children's education

In traditionally Buddhist Asian countries a child's schooling includes a basic outline of Buddhist values. The *Sigalovada Suttanta* gives five ways in which a pupil should conduct him- or herself towards the teacher, and five in which the teacher should conduct him- or herself towards the pupil.

The five devolving on the pupil are stated in Pali terms which may be construed literally and figuratively. In the literal sense, 1) the pupil should rise from his seat in salutation, 2) wait on the teacher, 3) desire to hear him, 4) render him personal service, and 5) honour him by reception. Figuratively these may be taken as displaying energy, understanding the teacher, paying attention, showing obedience, and preparing the work thoroughly.

The teacher should show his compassion, or love, for the pupils by teaching and training them well and happily, seeing that they grasp all the arts and crafts equally and thoroughly, teaching them in the respectful manner he adopts towards friends, and by making them secure in every way.

> (*Digha Nikaya*, Vol III, 189, quoted in H. Saddhatissa,
> *Buddhist Ethics*, Wisdom Publications, 1987, p 127)

In the West the situation is different:

Struggling to find our own way and balance in daily living – what about the children? Should we be establishing Buddhist schools? Some people are investigating this possibility and feel the need to provide a Buddhist orientated education. Others feel that the way forward is through integration. What is clear at the moment is that there is no form of western Buddhism to point to and say, 'This is how we will all do it'. True to the teachings themselves, everything is uncertain, but at this particular juncture in the development of Buddhism, incredibly exciting.

> (*World Religions in Education*, The Shap Working Party,
> 1986, p 23)

A Buddhist school has now been established for infants, at Brighton, in Sussex. Summer schools and family days are run by various Buddhist groups. The following extract from a children's newsletter illustrates the sort of activities that take place, in the words of a 9-year-old child:

A Day at Amaravati

A nun told us a story about a monkey, an elephant and a partridge. They tried to remember a tree to see who was the oldest and it was the partridge because he could remember he dropped the seed that grew into the tree.

We did paintings and drawings of that and after that we went out to the Stupa in the field and we had a joss stick each and held it like a prayer and we had to walk around three times and each time we came to the front we did three bows and then we stuck the joss sticks in the ground near the flowers and lit them . . . Then we did meditation. Ven. Amaro lit a candle and we sat cross-legged with our knees on the ground and were very quiet and looked at the candle and thought about who was our best friend and I thought I couldn't really say my brother because he is my best friend, so I thought about Charlie instead and then I thought of my brother who I love and my mummy and daddy and then Ven. Amaro banged a little gong and we woke up.

(*Rainbows Magazine*, No. 7, Amaravati Publications, 1986)

Children at an FWBO Buddha Day festival in Brighton

There is some debate as to how western Buddhist groups should educate their children, as one Buddhist observes:

Parents think different things about what we should do. Some think it should be like a Buddhist Sunday school. Others think we should leave them completely alone. My view is that I don't want to inject children with adult ideas. I want them to grow up with some healthy appreciation of the law of karma, of cause and effect; a healthy appreciation of others and that there is more to life than the material surface. There's a depth to life. What I don't want is a dead Dharma being injected in some way into children.

(FWBO member)

Death and dying

Death and dying are of particular significance in the Buddhist world view, because they are part of the cycle of rebirth, and therefore directly connected to birth itself (rather than being at the other end of life's events). It is important to die well, but also to live every moment as if it were one's last. This is not a morbid outlook. As one Tibetan teacher has said, 'Death is a great adventure'. Of course, fear of death *does* induce morbidity, and Buddhism addresses this issue. All is impermanent in the samsaric realm, and we must accept that. Rebirth is a consequence of this impermanence. Death is the event in the chain of cause and effect that induces rebirth. Sogyal Rimpoche, a Tibetan Lama who has written on the subject of death and dying, examines the issue thus:

At the moment of death our life becomes clear. Death is our greatest teacher. But, unfortunately, people in the West think of death only when they are dying. That is a little bit late.

He also makes the point that,

Life is nothing but changes, which are little deaths.
(Interview in the *Observer* newspaper, 22/11/92 p 55)

These teachings are complimented by Ajahn Sumedho in talking about Khamma (Kharma) and Rebirth.

By being mindful we free ourselves from the burden of birth and death, the habitually recreating pattern of khamma and rebirth. We recognise the boring, habitual re-creations of unsatisfactoriness, the obsessions with worry, doubt, fear, greed, hatred and delusion in all its forms. When we're mindful, there's no attachment to ideas and memories of self, and creativity is spontaneous.

(Ajahn Sumedho, *Cittaviveka*, Amaravati Publications, 1987, p 92)

Cleverness, of course, is concerned with how we make progress in the world in our present lifetime. Wisdom is about how we understand the prospect of living well in a wider context. And perhaps the advice given to Siddhartha by the Buddha in Herman Hesse's book is directly applicable here: 'Cleverness is good, but patience is better.'

This points to the need to accept and learn from the inevitable results of our Karma, of which impermanence and dying are a part. In *The Tibetan Book of the Dead*, an account of how to approach death, and the journey to rebirth, emphasise this event as a creative and practical process focused on mindfulness, through which ignorance can be overcome.

Such a positive approach to the inevitable event of death complements the work of hospice movements, and is borne out in Sogyal Rimpoche's statement that what we need to ask is, 'How can I help someone who is dying?' and 'Can you help someone who has already died?'

Funeral rites

When a person is dying it is usual for a monk or lay person to recite appropriate scriptures to them, to remind them of the Buddha's teaching and to calm their mind. In Tibetan Buddhism *The Tibetan Book of the Dead* is often read to prepare the dying person for the journey through the Bardo state, from this life to the next, with the hope that it will result in either liberation or a meritorious rebirth. It is important for the dying person to know that the state of mind in which they die will influence their rebirth.

At funerals, monks conduct the services, giving a talk and chanting scriptures on the theme of impermanence and the transitory nature of life. The ceremony does not dwell on bereavement, but on the qualities of the dead person. In the Soto Zen tradition the funeral is an ordination ceremony, in which the dead person's faith can be strengthened to help him or her face the Eternal Buddha without fear.

The relatives of the deceased person have a duty to arrange a memorial service with an alms offering at a temple or a monastery, or at home. This ceremony is meant to confer the transfer of merit to the deceased person. On anniversaries of death similar ceremonies may also be arranged. Relatives may also make gifts of money, books or objects to the temple or monastery.

The usual way of disposing of the body is by cremation. When great teachers die it is usual to preserve their relics in the same way as the Buddha's, and to distribute them to monasteries or centres set up by that teacher, where a *stupa* will be built to house them. These may then become centres of pilgrimage and be regarded as holy shrines. This has been done recently with two teachers who established branches of the Buddhist tradition in the West: the Thai teacher Ajahn Chah and the Tibetan Lama Yeshe. In both cases, relics and stupas can be found at centres which they founded in western countries.

Chorten (stupa) at Sarnath

Ajahn Chah's Funeral

On 16 January 1993 the body of Ajahn Chah was burned in a beautiful furnace specially built at the monastery where he had lived and taught. It was inside a great white circular building called a chedi or stupa which had a large arched doorway facing each of the four directions.

People came from all over the country and from abroad to climb the steps and go inside the stupa to see the ornate mother-of-pearl coffin in which Ajahn Chah's body had been kept for exactly a year since he died. (It had been specially treated so that it would keep that long and give everyone a chance to pay their respects to such a special person.)

Nearly half a million people including the King of Thailand, the Sangharaj (the head of the Thai Sangha) and Luang Por Sumedho assembled by the stupa to chant blessings, listen to talks, and sit in quiet reflection for many hours that day and night. At midnight the furnace was lit and many climbed the steps to see this final moment of Ajahn Chah's physical existence. White smoke curled out of the top of the tower on the stupa and drifted into the sky.

(*Rainbows Magazine*, Amaravati Publications, 1993, p 3)

After three days, a chosen number of bhikkhus presided over the extraction of the relics from the crematory. Most were locked up for safe-keeping; three large relics, white and honeycombed like coral, were placed on the shrine for public view. When we left, the Sangha were still using the chedi for their group meditation practice.

(*Forest Sangha Newsletter*, Amaravati Publications, Number 234, April 1993, p 5)

Rebirth

In the Tibetan tradition, when a great teacher dies, a search is made for his *tulku*, or reincarnation, at the request of the Dalai Lama. Lama Yeshe's tulku was found to be the son of two of his Spanish disciples. Once this identity is established the child will be brought up and educated according to Tibetan practice, in the belief that he will continue the work he performed in his previous life.

The procedure for finding a tulku is established in Tibetan lore. This account of the search for the present Dalai Lama (the fourteenth) serves as an example.

Lama Yeshe and his tulku
(Copyright Peter Gold. Photos reproduced from *Tibetan Reflections* with permission of
Wisdom Publications, 361 Newbury Street, Boston, Massachusetts, USA.)

Searching for the Dalai Lama

After certain signs had been observed as to the direction and location
in which he would be found, over a period of two years, and official
group was sent out to find him. They carried with them objects that
belonged to the thirteenth Dalai Lama. They disguised themselves
and visited houses in which they might find the child. Eventually
they came to a house that corresponded to one seen in a vision of the
Regent concerning the child. The two-year-old boy in the house was
subjected to the prescribed examination:

> He was first shown four different rosaries, one of which – the
> most worn – had belonged to the thirteenth Dalai Lama. The
> boy, who was quite unconstrained and not the least bit shy,
> chose the right one without hesitation and danced round the
> room with it. He also selected out of several drums one which the
> last Incarnation had used to call his servants. Then he took an
> old walking-stick, which had also belonged to him, not deigning

to bestow a glance on one which had a handle of ivory and silver.
(Heinrich Harrer, *Seven Years in Tibet*, Rupert Hart-Davies,
1953, pp269–70)

In this way the present Dalai Lama was found.

The idea that the dying teacher knows of his own rebirth is part of the uncanny logic of this whole process, to which we cannot all be privy. When Lama Yeshe met the parents of his tulku, prior to his death, he is said to have given a small pearl to the mother with the words, 'this is for your next child'.

'But I have enough children already,' she replied, 'I shan't be having another, fifth child.'

He gave her the pearl saying, 'Just in case, wait and see.'

9
FESTIVALS AND ___ CEREMONIES

There is great diversity in the range of Buddhist festivals and ceremonies because Buddhism has spread into a number of very different cultures in the course of its history. Nevertheless, they tend to focus on the Buddha Sakyamuni, the significant events in his life, his teachings and the Buddhist community. What differs is the way in which these events are celebrated, for each culture brings to them its own particular style and form and a specific calendar year. For this reason, it is best to divide Buddhist festivals into four main groups, representing the Theravada tradition; the Tibetan tradition; the Chinese-Japanese tradition and the Western Buddhist Order.

All Buddhist religious festivals follow the lunar calendar, and most of the important ones are celebrated on full-moon days. Knowing exactly when a particular festival will occur is not such an easy task. The solar calendar varies year by year, so just like Easter in the Christian tradition, Buddhist festival days fall on moveable dates. Buddhists rely on printed calendars for their information, and the festival celebration itself will occur on the appropriate full-moon day (or sometimes on the weekend closest to it in non-Buddhist countries).

Theravada festivals

The traditional importance of monastic orders in Buddhism has a strong influence on the character of Theravada festivals. The monastic calendar is marked by two important events: *uposatta* days, which occur weekly, and the Rains Retreat, which occurs annually. Devout lay people may also follow the monks' observance of uposatta days.

Uposatta days

Originally, uposatta days were times when monks met on the full moon and new moon to re-affirm their monastic code and confess their shortcomings to one another. They subsequently developed into days of religious observance for lay people as well. Occurring weekly, they function in a similar way to the Sabbath in Judeo-Christian practice, but since the full moon is the most auspicious day, (because it marks the Buddha's birth, enlightenment and death), this is treated as far more important than the others, with the new moon also being more significant than the other two.

It is worth noting how full-moon observance actually keeps Buddhists in touch with natural rhythms as well; this is not just coincidental, for samsara is a notion that unites the cycles of the natural world with those of human destiny. The moon acts as a symbolic reminder of both the samsaric round of human life and the presence of the Dharma, or truth made available by the Buddha, which is also ever-present. Thus the full moon gains a magical quality, pointing to the need for diligence and offering the hope of liberation.

The pattern of observance on these days involves visiting a monastery or temple, listening to the teaching given by a monk, chanting from the scriptures, taking part in meditation and re-affirming the precepts. For a devout lay person this is an opportunity to gain merit by performing acts of generosity, donating money to the monastery and showing reverence to the Buddha, through performing acts of devotion before Buddha images. Another common practice is to take the Eight Precepts for the day, rather than the usual five, and to pursue the precepts more diligently. So, for example, they may abstain from eating meat or fish, practise sexual abstinence, not eat after noon or forego the use of adornments and usual forms of entertainment. In short, they are re-acquainting themselves with the renunciant life, behaving temporarily like members of the monastic order. Buddhist festivals tend to be less a matter of festivity, more a matter of remembrance and re-affirmation.

New Year

Occurring on 13 April (western calendar) in Sri Lanka and Thailand, but on the 16 April in Burma, this festival is really secular, and often somewhat irreverent, but socially significant. In Sri Lanka it operates rather like the western Christmas. It is a time for visiting relatives and friends and giving presents; in Burma and in Laos people buy and release fish as an act of compassion. In Thailand it is a water-throwing festival. Veneration is also shown to Buddha images, revered teachers and respected grandfathers, by sprinkling or bathing them with water. The festivities continue for three days. Temporary sand stupas are erected in temple grounds, which are later levelled to create new sand surfaces. Robes are placed on Buddha images and are used afterwards by the monks. Pranks are also played, for it has its light-hearted side.

Wesak

Wesak celebrates the Buddha's birth, enlightenment and death, which are all, according to Buddhist tradition, supposed to have occurred on the same day of the year; as such, this is the most important Theravadin festival. It takes place on the full moon day of the second month in the Indian year, which, in the western calendar, occurs in late May or early June. The Indian name for this month is Vaishakha, which, translated into Sinhalese, becomes Wesak, and in Thai, Visakha. Thus the festival is named after the month. Emphasis is placed on the enlightenment of the Buddha, which is the pre-eminent event, since it marks the point at which the Dharma was rediscovered by the historical Buddha Sakyamuni. It is customary to put up decorations in local temples and to light lamps after dark, symbolising enlightenment coming into the world. Wesak lanterns are made by pasting thin paper over light wooden frames. At temples Bodhi trees and stupas are often ringed with oil lamps, and people send Wesak cards to their friends, rather like Christmas cards. These usually depict memorable events in the Buddha's life.

Other activities are reminiscent of lesser Buddhist festivals, with lay people visiting local temples or monasteries, listening to darsanas and staying up through the night in meditation. In the Thai tradition, it is customary to circumambulate the monastery three times, recognising the importance of the Buddha, Dharma and Sangha (the Three Jewels). Observance of the precepts in a more rigorous way also entails abstaining from agriculture or other occupations which may harm small living creatures. Dana (generosity) is also encouraged, which results in lay families often bringing sumptuous dishes to the monastery or temple in recognition of their duty to the monastic order, and as a further way of expressing the festive spirit of the occasion and the importance of the whole Sangha. This also confers merit.

In Burma, though it is not recognised as a festival of light, as in Sri Lanka, the importance of the occasion is marked by watering the Bodhi tree in a local monastery or temple.

At this point it is worth reflecting on the significance of festivals for Buddhists; which do not necessarily parallel their importance in the Christian tradition. For example, even the pre-eminent festival of Wesak is not necessarily seen as of great importance for Buddhists, in the context of striving for enlightenment and moral improvement, as the following passage indicates:

> Wesak is all right: it's a day which commemorates the birth, the Enlightenment, and the passing away of the Buddha. But why make extra effort for one particular day? For the feeble-minded, perhaps a day like that would be of much benefit. But to me, every day should be a day of effort – should be such a day. Why just one particular day?
>
> (John Bowker, *Worlds of Faith*, BBC, 1983, p 159)

A Buddhist family at Wesak with *dana* for the monks and nuns

Poson

This is a peculiarly Sri Lankan festival which occurs on the next full moon day after Wesak, in June or July. On this day, in the year 250 BCE, the emperor Ashoka's son, Mahinda, who was a Buddhist monk, is supposed to have arrived in Sri Lanka to convert the island to Buddhism. Religious processions, called *perahara*, are organised, in which a particularly venerated person or object is conducted through the town, with great pomp and noise made especially with drums and fireworks. Often an image of Mahinda is constructed and placed on a cart or float-like vehicle. At Mihintale, near the ancient capital of Anapurna, where Mahinda is said to have arrived, these festivities are at their grandest.

Asala

Asala, normally in July, marks the beginning of the Rains Retreat (called Vas in Sinhalese) and recalls the preaching of the Buddha's first sermon, the Turning of the Wheel of the Law. Since this marks the beginning of the Buddha's ministry, monks preach sermons recalling the event. In the latter half of the month Sri Lankans stage the Asola Perahara, a spectacular procession in which the relic of the Buddha's tooth is processed through the streets of Kandy. Relics of the Buddha, or of great Buddhist teachers, are usually to be found wherever Buddhist missionary activity has founded new centres. But the history of this event is primarily nationalistic rather than religious. This ceremony marks the importance of Buddhist identity within Sinhalese nationalism, acting as a display of the legitimacy of the power of the king. The legacy of this is a contemporary exhibition of a distinctively Sri Lankan festival, with sumptuously decorated elephants, dancers, festivity and fireworks that have the character of a mardi-gras. It is a local pageant which really has little to do with Buddhist ideals and is the prerogative of the laity rather than monks.

Rains Retreat

The Buddha preached and spent his life travelling northern India and throughout the subcontinent in general. Life is regulated between the months of June or July through to the end of September by the monsoon season. Travel during this season was, at the least, uncomfortable and often practically impossible. It became a habitual practice that during these periods wandering monks would settle down in one sheltered place. This developed into the strict monastic rule that monks would not leave their monastery during this period, and this provided a time for more intense devotional practice. Correspondingly, today the normal availability of monks to the laity is curtailed.

At the end of the retreat, monks hold a special ceremony confessing any fault or offence, and asking forgiveness of their fellow order members. On the final day of the retreat, or within the following month, the relationship with the laity is re-established with the Kathina ceremony.

In Burma and Thailand lay men often take temporary ordination at the beginning of the retreat and live as monks for the next three months. There are also no Burmese weddings during this period. At the end of the retreat the Burmese celebrate the festival of Thitingyut, which lasts three days and is their festival of lights. Everyone is expected to visit elder relations and friends, to pay respects and give small gifts. Lamps are put up (traditionally consisting of candles inside paper lanterns) all over the house and on shrines of local deities, (nats), in big trees, which are specially venerated, and around stupas. The lights are said to illuminate and welcome the Buddha's descent from heaven after preaching to his mother. In Thailand lay people use candles to light lamps in the monastery, which will burn for the three months of the retreat.

Kathina ceremony

Held in October or November of the western calendar, Kathina is organised by lay people in order to present monks with new robes. One robe is ceremonially presented as the Kathina robe to the head of the monastery, to be given to the monk who is, at least in theory, to be the most virtuous. He will be chosen by the abbot. This story illustrates the origins of the practice:

> The scriptures relate that thirty monks were travelling together with the intention of spending the retreat season with the Buddha. However, when the full moon of July (the start of the retreat) arrived, they had not reached their destination, and according to custom they were required to stay where they were. So, it is told, the monks were disappointed, and spent the three-month retreat away from their teacher.
>
> At the end of the retreat the monks finished their journey to see the Buddha. Coming to hear of their disappointment, he was

moved to give them a teaching that would uplift and inspire them. He suggested that they should make a new robe together. The lay supporters living near the Buddha gladly offered cloth and the monks set about sewing a robe. In those days the method used involved spreading the pieces of cloth on a frame and stitching them together. This frame was called a *kathina*.

(Bhikkhu Thitapanne, *The Kathina Festival*, in C. Erricker and V. Barnett (eds), *World Religions in Education: Festivals*, The Shap Working Party, 1987, p 21)

The robe is made according to ceremonial prescription, by sewing patches together in such a way as is said to imitate the patchwork of the paddy fields familiar to the early monks on their travels. The community first presents the cloth for the robe, which is marked, cut out and sewn by the monks on the same day, before being given back to the laity for presentation. Another meaning given to the word 'kathina' is 'difficult', which suggests the arduousness of the vocation of a disciple of the Buddha, and the tenacity required to follow the Dhamma.

The robe-giving ceremony is also a reminder of the interdependence of the monastic order and the laity; the monks offer spiritual example and teaching to lay followers and, in return, the laity satisfy the mendicants' basic needs. This interdependence was stressed by the Buddha, and has certainly been a vital factor in the survival and continuation of Buddhism as a living tradition. Its importance is highlighted by the fact that this ceremony is the only one involving the laity that gains its authority from the earliest Buddhist scriptures.

This sensitive description of the robe-giving ceremony, by a British Buddhist, conveys its essential meaning:

Now began one of the simplest and most moving ceremonies that I have been privileged to witness. The Kathina robe was presented on its own special stand in front of the Shrine and the resident Bhikkhu was invited to receive it. The reverence of the ritual by which the recipient made that robe his own shed a whole new light on the significance and virtue of giving. The robe was unwrapped and examined as if each fold and thread was to be personally known.

Next the robe was marked in one corner. The significance of this action has been lost over the years. It could be that the marks were originally a means of identifying the robe, serving the purpose of a name tag. Or it is possibly a deliberate defacing of the newness of the robe, making it come with built-in wear and tear and therefore, losing the sense of pride that new things invariably bring. Finally, the new robe was placed between the folds of the old robe and the two were stroked together. The symbolism of this action was as if the one was being made a natural continuation of the other. The new robe became endowed with the qualities of the old – the one was never actually cast aside and the other never actually replacing. The two merged as a continuance of purpose.

(Gwen Nodder, *First Make Your Shrine*, in C. Erricker and V. Barnett (eds), *World Religions in Education: Festivals*, The Shap Working Party, 1987, pp 22–3)

Burmese custom emphasises that girls weave the monks' robes. Along with the robes, toy trees are offered, representing the mythical trees of heaven. On their branches the lay people pin banknotes, as an offering to the monastery.

Ajahn Sumedho, a Theravadin monk, wearing robes

Loi Kratong

This is the main Thai festival of lights, held on the full moon of November. Like Asala in Sri Lanka, this is not centred on the temple, and has only tenuous connections with Buddhist origins. Gates and doors of houses are decorated with palm leaves, banana stalks, coloured lanterns, lamps and candles. The monastery grounds are similarly decorated with paper flags and sets depicting scenes from the *Vessantara Jataka* recalling the previous life of the Buddha as the compassionate Prince Vessantara, and his selfless generosity. There are also offerings to the river spirits, consisting of floating trays with lighted candles, coins and food. In return for these the spirits will rid people of misfortunes. These offerings are processed to the rivers accompanied by fireworks, drums and gongs. The river comes alive, the variety of craft launched upon it ranging from huge floats to tiny trays of plaited banana leaves.

Magha Puja

This Thai festival marks All Saints' Day, or Dharma Day. It commemorates an event three months before the Buddha's death when, before 1,250 of his enlightened disciples, he predicted his demise and gave them the *Vinaya* (the code of discipline for the monastic Sangha), which all monks are now supposed to recite every fortnight. In Northern Thailand and Laos this day is the festival of lights, when the *Vessantara Jataka* is read through in one day. It is also marked by a great fair.

Tibetan festivals

Tibet provides a distinctive culture for Buddhist life, and the terms 'Tibetan' and 'Buddhist' are synonymous within the Tibetan world. Before the invasion of Tibet by China in 1959, little was known of this way of life, but since then, Tibetan Buddhism has established itself in India and across Europe and the United States, with the diaspora led by the present, fourteenth, Dalai Lama and a number of important Buddhist teachers, or lamas, around whom communities have grown. The centre of 'Tibet in exile' is the small town of McLeod Gange, above Dharamsala in the Indian foothills of the Himalayas, where the Dalai Lama has his palace.

The Tibetan calendar is lunar and divided into twelve months; to keep in step with the solar year it is necessary to add a month during certain years. To keep in phase with the moon some months are less than thirty days. Some Tibetan festivals commemorate the usual events related to the Buddha's life; others have a peculiarly Tibetan significance.

Losar

Losar is Tibetan New Year, which falls in February. Lasting for fifteen days, it commemorates the Buddha's early life, through to his enlightenment and his efforts to establish the Dharma during his teaching career. Within Tibet monks sat their examinations for higher degrees on the fourth day, called the Great Prayer (Monlam Cheamo). The fifteenth day is the full moon day, Chonga Chopa, when Tibetan culture comes into its own with the remarkable butter sculptures for which it is famous. These are usually of scenes in the Buddha's life, coloured with different dyes. Tibetans also put on puppet shows on the same themes. Traditionally, the monks of two famous monasteries called the Upper Tantric School (Gyuto) and Lower Tantric School (Gyume) are responsible for these displays. They are now located in India, and the celebrations take place in Dharamsala.

The sense of the New Year as a time of trial and conquest in the Buddha's life is echoed in the Tibetans' understanding of its significance for them. It is a time of overcoming and renewal, as this commentary on its rituals and celebrations taking place at Dharamsala shows:

> The New Year must be borne decisively from out of the ashes of the old. Negative thoughts, deeds, and misfortunes accumulated during the previous year are purged from community, home, and individual lives through prescribed rituals by clergy and members of the household.
>
> The ushering in of *losar*, the New Year, begins on the evening of the twenty-ninth day of the last month of the old year. Tibetan friends and family gather together to partake of *gutuk*, the 'special nine soups'. Contained within are sculpted and stuffed dumplings, which signify the fortunes for the coming year of every person present. The person who chooses a dumpling stuffed with salt might gain renown and lead a virtuous life during the coming twelve moons. Whoever gets the chilli

pepper will be angry and argumentative. And woe be it to he or she with the lump of charcoal, for that person will be cursed with a black heart. This provides many laughs for most and frowns for a few.

Each person finishes all but a little of his soup. The leftovers, along with old food, coins, pieces of clothing lint, a candle, and a *khatag* greeting-scarf are put together into a large bowl along with a humanoid-shaped *torma* sculpture known as *lu*. These serve as ransom offerings to attract the accrued evil and misfortune of the past year away from the household. The men carry the items to a lonely spot along the road by torchlight, crying 'Come out! Come out!' to the evils. The job done, they quickly return without ever looking back, for to do so would cause the evil to return with them. This act, it occurs to me, is a powerful metaphor to a central notion in the Tibetan experience, that one must continue on life's path without looking back. 'No attachments, no regrets', a lama once observed.

(Peter Gold, *Tibetan Reflections*, Wisdom Publications, 1984, pp 82–3)

Following this, a procession of monks carries special New Year *zor tormas*, which are huge constructions in which the community's bad karma of the previous year is symbolically enclosed by ritual prayers. On top of these conical edifices are death's heads. The torma is paraded towards a large mound of straw, a pyre on which the physical manifestation of evil will be burned.

Tibetan New Year has its own special place in the calendar and, as on other celebratory occasions, the Tibetan love of colour and ritual is evidenced by an abundance of coloured prayer flags and the sounds of Tibetan instruments.

Saga Dawa

This festival, held on the fifteenth day of the fourth month (the full moon of May in the gregorian or western calendar), recognises the Buddha's birth, enlightenment and death (the equivalent of Wesak). This is the strictest observance day in the Tibetan calendar, when no meat is eaten and lamps are lit everywhere. Circumambulation is another feature of this festival; devotion is shown by going round Buddhist monuments in a clockwise direction, by means of prostration – measuring out the distance with the body and standing where the head faced the ground in a continuously repeated process. Devout

Buddhists will also take a vow to fast and be silent for seven days, which symbolises both the significance of abstinence in Buddhist practice and the Buddha's passing.

Dzamling Chisang

This is a day of purification which falls on the full moon day of the fifth month (June). Fire offerings are made to guardian spirits who protect individuals, families and places of importance and who act as national deities. Shrines are erected next to Buddhist temples. Tibetan belief in spirits goes back to their bon ancestry (the indigenous religion preceding Buddhism). The spirits are seen as having been converted to Buddhism and becoming its protectors. Since they are vegetarian, burnt offerings are made of favourite Tibetan dishes such as roast barley mixed with butter, and Tibetan sweets. The offerings are made by lay people, who abstain from meat for three days beforehand.

Chokhor

This festival commemorates the Buddha's first sermon, the Turning of the Wheel of the Law. Occurring in June or July, on the fourth day of the sixth month, it is a summer festival, associated in the Tibetan climate with fine weather and colourful celebration. The community would carry *xylographs*, scriptures engraved on long, rectangular wooden blocks, and statues, in great processions with a carnival atmosphere. This signified the spread of the Dharma through the Buddha's teaching. Afterwards there would be picnics, often with traditional Tibetan brew of *chang*, an equivalent of beer based on the fermenting of wheat, which facilitated hospitality and festivity.

Lhabap

On the twenty-second of the ninth month (October), Tibetans celebrate the Buddha's descent from the Tushita heaven where he preached to his mother. It occurs at the same time as the end of the Rains Retreat in Theravada countries. It represents his return to earth, when temples are visited and feasts occur.

Ngacho Chenmo

This event is the anniversary of the death of Tsongkhapa on the twenty-fifth day of the tenth month, falling in November. Tsongkhapa founded the Yellow Hat school of Tibetan Buddhism, which includes the Upper and Lower Tantric Schools. Possibly the most influential figure in Tibetan Buddhism, Tsongkhapa, was a monk famous for his learning and the strictness of his monastic discipline. As a mark of mourning Tibetans eat a special porridge containing lumps of dough, and lamps are lit in his memory. In Lhasa, his image used to be carried in a torchlight procession. This day also marks the end of the Rains Retreat period, when new robes are offered to monks.

Guru Rimpoche's birthday

Guru Rimpoche's birthday occurs in July, and celebrates one of the greatest of Tibetan figures. The title means 'precious teacher', and was given to Padmasambhava, who converted many Tibetans to the practice of Buddhism as one of the first Indians to bring the Dharma to Tibet. It is celebrated with a Tsok ceremony; food and light are offered to the Buddha in beautifully decorated shrine rooms in which highly colourful pictures, known as *thangkas*, hang round the walls, and statues of Buddhas are placed around the room. Flowers and incense also create a celebratory atmosphere, in which chanting and silent meditation take place. At the end of the ceremony food which has been offered is shared amongst the worshippers.

The following description of a statue of the guru in the Himalayan hillside around Dharamsala recalls his significance for Tibetan Buddhists:

> A huge, glaring statue of the *guru* himself sits carved into eighteen feet of gilded rock. A *dorje* (thunderbolt-scepter) is held incisively in one hand, skull staff in the other. Huge eyes pierce one with the legendary power he manifested to the independent mountain people to the north, powerful enough to consolidate their beliefs and enlist their native gods into a distinctively Tibetan form of Buddhism.
>
> (Peter Gold, *Tibetan Reflections*, Wisdom Publications, 1984, p 76)

Stories of Padmasambhava recall his great power, and sometimes miraculous feats, as with this episode occurring in the present-day Indian village of Rewalsar.

There he meditated in a cave high over a massive valley, and took one of the local king's daughters as his consort. The king of Zahor, being angered by his daughter's uncomely behaviour, condemned Padmasambhava to be burned alive. The fire was ignited but he was not even scorched. And the flames, turning into water, overspilled to form a beautiful oval lake which Tibetans call *Tsopema*, the Lotus Lake.

(Peter Gold, *Tibetan Reflections*, Wisdom Publications, 1984, p 75)

Japanese and Chinese festivals

Buddhist influence has waned in China since its peak a thousand years ago, when it combined with Taoist and Confucian indigenous tradition. In recent history, the Maoist revolution and China's present communist government have repressed Buddhist practice, but not eradicated it. It still survives, particularly in the provinces close to Tibet. Though the western calendar is influential today, the Chinese still use lunar months, which operate in a similar way to the Tibetan system. Chinese tradition is especially concerned with the remembrance of dead ancestors and the celebration of birthdays, and this influences their Buddhist festivals.

Japan received Buddhism via China, so it is not surprising to find similarities, though variations of Buddhism in Japan have flourished in connection with Shinto, the earlier Japanese religion (which bears similarity with Confucianism in its respect for ancestors, and filial and state order are of great importance). The two main festivals in both countries share common themes. The names referred to here are the Japanese versions.

Gautama Buddha's birth

This is known as Hana Matsuri in Japan, where the Buddha's enlightenment and death are remembered separately. It occurs on 8 April, and, correspondingly in the Chinese calendar, on the eighth day of the fourth month. The themes of flowers and water are prevalent, reflecting the mythology of the Buddha's birth itself:

> The beautiful queen Mahamaya had a dream. She saw a young white elephant with six great tusks descend from the sky and enter her womb. The gods told her that she was going to give

birth to a son which would become a buddha. The queen told her husband the news and they were both very happy. When the time for the birth of the child was close, the queen decided to travel to her parents' house, as was the custom at that time. On the way she visited a beautiful garden called Lumbini Grove. The garden was full of flowers and singing birds. Suddenly, the queen started to give birth and so the Buddha was born in a beautiful, flowering garden.

After the birth two streams of water appeared from the sky. One was cool and refreshing; the other was warm and perfumed. They bathed the Buddha and his mother.

The infant Buddha stood up as soon as he was born. Shaded by a white parasol held over him by the gods, he faced north and took seven steps. Then, looking in each of the other directions, he said, 'I am the chief in the world, I am the best in the world. This is my last birth, I will not be born again.'

(Peter and Holly Connolly, *Religions Through Festivals: Buddhism*, Longman, 1989, p 32)

At Japanese temples different aspects of the story are shown in displays.

A large papier-mâché white elephant reminds people of the queen's marvellous dream. The infant Buddha stands, to remind people that he could walk as soon as he was born and the setting represents the Lumbini Grove. Bowls of delicately perfumed tea are poured on to the Buddha's image by Japanese Buddhist children. This is a way of honouring the Buddha and remembering that the gods provided perfumed water from heaven for his first bath.

(Peter and Holly Connolly, *Religions Through Festivals: Buddhism*, Longman, 1989, p 33)

The festival coincides with the flowering of the cherry blossom in Japan, and stalls selling food and gifts are set up in temple courtyards. Folk dancing and acrobatics form part of the celebrations.

The following description of a Chinese ceremony also recalls the bathing of the Buddha by the gods.

After hymns and offerings the monks poured spoonfuls of water over a tiny image of the infant Sakyamuni, standing in a low basin of water. Sometimes each of the [lay] visitors was allowed to pour a spoonful too.

(Holmes Welch, *The Practice of Chinese Buddhism*, quoted in Alan Brown (ed.), *Festivals in World Religions*, Longman, 1986, pp 5–58)

The Festival of the Hungry Ghosts

This festival honours dead ancestors. According to Buddhist cosmology, samsara is divided into realms, through which living beings pass. The realm of the hungry ghosts is one of these. In effect it parallels All Soul's Day, but with special significance due to the importance of ancestors in Japanese and Chinese tradition. Occurring in July, or the seventh month in the Chinese calendar, (July or August), it lasts for three and seven days, in Japan and China respectively. It recalls the story of Maudgalyayana, or Mu-lien, one of the Buddha's chief disciples who had special powers, through which he was able to visit other realms. On one of his journeys he found his mother in one of the hells. In some versions she is described as one of the hungry ghosts, who typically suffer from distended stomachs and tiny mouths (illustrating their incapacity to satisfy their desires). The story recounts that he saved her by offering a feast to all Buddhas and monks, and by virtue of this act of merit she was raised out of hell by the Buddha using a rope.

The theme of this story is mirrored in the following Chinese ceremony of the 'release of the burning mouths', performed on the full moon day.

> This was a Tantric ritual lasting about five hours and always held in the evening when it was easier for hungry ghosts to go abroad. The presiding monks wore red and golden hats in the shape of a five-pointed crown. Before them was a collection of magical instruments – mirrors, sceptres, spoons, and so on. The monks assisting them – usually six to eighteen – were equipped with . . . bells (which sounded, when rung together, rather like a team of reindeer). In the first half of the ceremony the celebrants invoked the help of the Three Jewels. In the second half they broke through the gates of hell, where, with their instruments and magic gestures, they opened the throats of the sufferers and fed them sweet dew, that is, water made holy by reciting a [prayer] over it. They purged away their sins, administered the Three Refuges [declaring one's trust in the Three Jewels], and caused them to take the Bodhisattva resolve. Finally they preached the *dharma* [the Buddha's teachings] to them. If all this was properly done, the ghosts could be immediately reborn as men or even in the Western Paradise.
>
> (Holmes Welch, *The Practice of Chinese Buddhism*, quoted in Alan Brown (ed.), *Festivals in World Religions*, Longman, 1986, p 57)

In Japan fairs take place with food, shows, dancing and games – especially tug-of-war, a reminder to them of the Maudagalyayana story. Ancient Japanese customs are included. On the first day of the festival, 13 July, freshly gathered herbs are placed in front of the family shrine, candles are lit and food is offered to attract the spirits of ancestors into the homes. On 14 July families celebrate the reunion of their ancestors with the living with traditional folk dances. Buddhist monks visit homes and read scriptures before the shrines as a mark of respect. On 15 July the spirits return to the other realms, and fruit and flowers are offered to the Buddha with requests for blessings on the family and ancestors in future life.

Western Buddhist festivals

The Friends of the Western Buddhist Order celebrate the Buddhist year with three main festivals: Buddha Day, Dharma Day and Sangha Day, representing the Three Jewels.

Buddha Day is held on the full moon in May, and celebrates the Buddha's enlightenment. Dharma Day is in July, and Sangha Day in November, according with Kathina. These are times for the Western Buddhist Order to come together with friends or *mitras*, interested westerners are also welcome. The gatherings take place in FWBO centres, which are usually large houses or halls converted to Buddhist purposes. Ceremonies take place in a shrine room, decorated for the occasion, and include a talk from a senior Order member, a puja with chanting and meditation, and the sharing of food. Sometimes special events are held for children. Mitra ceremonies are often held after the puja on Dharma Day, when new members of the community, wishing to affirm their commitment do so by taking the Three Jewels, and offer flowers, candles and incense in front of the shrine. On Sangha Day mitras make these same three offerings as a reaffirmation of their commitment.

Shrine at FWBO festival, Buddha Day.

10
BUDDHISM TODAY: EAST AND WEST

—— The spread of Buddhism ——

Today Buddhists are spread across the world; however, as with peoples of other faiths, such as Christianity, it is not always easy to identify them.

Buddhist monks and nuns, who have been ordained into the monastic Sangha, wear saffron robes if they belong to the South East Asian (Theravada) tradition, maroon robes if they are Tibetan, and black robes if they are Zen monks. However, their conspicuousness does not identify the far larger number of lay Buddhists. We might say that to identify monastics as the whole Buddhist community would be rather like identifying clergymen as the sole representatives of Christianity. Let us briefly consider the presence of Buddhism in Asia, the United Kingdom and the United States today.

Buddhism in Asia

Buddhism began in India but, for reasons which will be explained later, Buddhism eventually declined there and, through missionary activity, spread north, south and east. Today the tradition survives in India, largely through the conversion movement of Dr Ambedka amongst the Untouchables, (or, as Gandhi named them, *Harijans* – Children of God) which has expanded since its inception in 1956 to at least three and a half million. India also hosts the larger number of Tibetans in exile since the Chinese invasion of Tibet in 1959. (The

Dalai Lama's residence is situated in the small town of McLeod Gange, near Dharamsala in the Himalayan foothills, and this is regarded as the centre of Tibetan Buddhism whilst exile continues. Apart from Tibet, Buddhism still flourishes in Sri Lanka, Burma, Thailand and Japan, though political change has affected its presence in China, Korea, Cambodia and Vietnam – all of which have a strong history of Buddhist influence.

Buddhism in the West has emerged, partly through immigrant communities arriving in Europe and North America but also through westerners discovering Buddhism or becoming Buddhist monks in Asia and returning to the West as part of Buddhist missionary activity in the twentieth century.

Buddhism in the United Kingdom

Although Buddhist ideas were studied in late Victorian Britain, the religion was brought to public attention by a Buddhist monk, Ananda Metteyya (the Englishman Alan Bennett). The Buddhist Society of Great Britain and Ireland was founded in 1907 as a vehicle for his teaching. It was succeeded in 1924 by the present Buddhist Society, the founder president of which was the late Judge Christmas Humphreys, who largely created the climate in which Buddhism began to take root and flourish in the West. In 1926 the London Buddhist Vihara was established in Chiswick, West London – the earliest Buddhist temple in Britain.

Since that time, many different branches of Buddhism have been established, originating in such countries as Thailand, Tibet and Japan. As a result, Britain today has a great variety of Buddhist groups and communities – far more than would be found in any one 'traditionally Buddhist' country. The *Directory of Buddhist Groups*, produced by the Buddhist Society, reported 74 groups in 1979; eight years later there were 191, and this number continued to grow. The four largest are illustrated here.

The Theravada tradition is the branch of Buddhism predominant in South East Asia and Sri Lanka. In Britain there are a number of Theravadin communities. Those from Sir Lanka have their main centre at the London Buddhist Vihara (monastic residence). There is also a Thai Forest Retreat Order, established by the late Ajahn Chah, with its main activities at 'Amaravati', a Buddhist Monastery in Hertfordshire and 'Cittaviveka' in Sussex. the names 'Amaravati' (meaning 'deathless realm') and 'Cittaviveka' (meaning 'silent mind') give clues to the aspirations of all Buddhists. The monks and nuns in this order in Britain are western converts to Buddhism. There is also a Thai temple in the London area, as well as a Burmese vihara.

The Tibetan tradition has all four of its branches represented in Britain: the Manjushri Institute at Ulverstone, Cumbria, Samye-Ling Buddhist Centre at Eskdalemuire in Dumfriesshire, and the Madhyamika Centre, near York, are the largest.

The Japanese Soto-Zen tradition has a centre near Hexham in Northumberland and a smaller centre in Reading, Berkshire. There are also a number of affiliated groups around the country, known as Serene Reflection Meditation Groups.

The Friends of the Western Buddhist Order was established in Britain in 1967 by the Venerable Sangharakshita, an Englishman formerly called Dennis Lingwood. He believed that it was necessary to establish a form of Buddhism which was adapted to the circumstances of the modern world. The largest centre in Britain is the Buddhist Centre in Bethnal Green, East London.

Buddhism in the United States

In the United States Buddhist influence has been felt more keenly in certain areas than in other western countries. This is partly due to its proximity to Asia on the west coast. At the end of the nineteenth century, Japanese and Chinese families settled in California; the Japanese also settled in Hawaii during the twentieth century after the enforcement of strict immigration laws in California in 1902. Hawaii also became the focus of Buddhist missionary activity in the United States, which in turn led to temples and meditation centres being established on the mainland. In the process of this transference from their original cultural setting, Buddhists have adapted their organisations and forms of service. Buddhist influence has also spread into American cultural life, beyond classically Buddhist Institutions, through its attraction as a spiritual philosophy, and a meditative practice.

To some degree, the spread of Buddhism in the United States – especially along the west coast – has only a tentative relationship with the religion as it has developed in traditionally Buddhist countries, such as Japan. Young western liberals, anxious to find an alternative to establishment thinking, propagated Zen as a life-enhancing but essentially individualistic philosophy of life. This can be recognised, for example, in the writings of Alan Watts who (although British) lived and worked for the majority of his life in the United States, and was related to the beat movement of the late 1950s and early 1960s, typified by Jack Kerouac and Allen Ginsberg. Such love-affairs with Buddhist ideas, whilst exhilarating, could not be responsible for rooting Buddhism in a new culture. The seeds of Buddhism in America were more obviously sown as a result of the World Parliament of Religions in Chicago in 1893, where Anagarika Dharmapala spoke as founder of the Maha-Bodhi Society and as a practising Buddhist monk in the Theravada (South Asian) tradition.

The proliferation of Buddhist centres during the latter half of the twentieth century owes much to the work of established Japanese teachers, such as Shunryu Suzuki and his American disciple Richard Baker, who received his entitlement to teach from his Japanese master. By transferring this traditional lineage to a new socio-cultural environment, Buddhism may well establish a lasting presence on new soil whilst remaining true to its own principle of spreading the Dharma.

This discussion of the influence of Buddhism worldwide once again points to the importance of establishing a Sangha or Buddhist community, as the tradition spreads from one country to another. Taking account of the customs and *mores* of different societies is a recurring theme in Buddhism. Accordingly, we shall now investigate in greater detail the way in which three different forms of Buddhism have adapted to and influenced the modern world.

The Tibetan situation

Tibetan society

The single most dramatic historical event to have an effect on Buddhism in the twentieth century has been the Chinese invasion of Tibet, and the subsequent exile of the Dalai Lama in India since 1959. At this time Tibetan society was still feudal in nature, and half its six million population were nomadic. One third of its labour force worked on the land. The third largest group were the monks, fifteen per cent of the population. Otherwise, the most conspicuous group was professional beggars. This was a recognised way of life with set traditions. Because almsgiving was an obligation of the faithful, begging did not have the sort of disapprobation attached to it that we find in the West. One group of beggars (the *ragyapa*) was traditionally assigned the role of disposers of the dead. Corpses would be taken to nearby peaks, and cut up, with the flesh laid out and bones pulverised, so that they could be eaten by vultures and wild animals. Alternatively, the poor would be placed into swiftly flowing streams, to be eaten by the fish. In this way, the discarded body became food for fellow creatures. It was the performance of a generous and meritorious deed.

Only renowned teachers' and high lamas' bodies were treated differently. The formers' relics would be placed in *chortens* (stupas) as a memorial and reminder of their teachings. The latter would be embalmed by the monastic community.

Tibet had harboured no militaristic or expansionist ambitions in the previous 1,000 years of Buddhist influence. Its balance of payments with regard to imports against exports, such as they were, was healthy. It was, essentially, a highly conservative society that saw no need for change. Once villages had provided themselves with the physical necessities of life, any spare income was used in making offerings to temples and monasteries and the poor. There was no unemployment in the accepted sense, and social advancement did not fit the scheme of things. Since a century before Columbus, the ruler of Church and State had been the Dalai Lama, the first being born in a nomad's tent on the plains of eastern Tibet. The order of Tibetan society was ordained by the same law that decreed the Dalai Lama always to be an incarnation of the Bodhisattva Chenresig (Avalokiteshvara).

Today Tibet has been shaken by the political, military and social changes of Chinese insurgence. Monasteries have been destroyed, resistance has been systematically subjugated and, most significantly for Tibetans, the Dalai Lama himself is absent. Tibetan Buddhism in exile has had to consider its adaptation to a larger world.

Tibetan Buddhism in exile

The key figure in this adaptation is the Dalai Lama himself. Based in Dharamsala but travelling the world, he balances the twin needs of sustaining the fabric of Tibetan life in exile and acting as ambassador for its cause. At the same time he remains a Buddhist monk.

Ever since the invasion, His Holiness (as he is known to Tibetans) has appealed to the United Nations on the question of Tibet. This has resulted in three resolutions being adopted by the General Assembly, but China has repeatedly refused to respond positively to the various proposals offered to alleviate the Tibetan situation. It is remarkable, and yet consistent, that the policies advocated by the Dalai Lama to solve the Tibetan problem have always been based on non-violence. This gained him worldwide recognition in 1989 when he was awarded the Nobel Peace Prize. However, it has not resulted in substantial political backing from the international community. The Dalai Lama's concern for the plight of Tibetans remaining in their mother country is made clear in the following statement:

> On this anniversary, I pay homage to the brave men and women of Tibet, who laid down their lives for the freedom of our country, and I call upon every Tibetan to renew our dedication until we have regained our rights and freedom.
>
> (*His Holiness the Dalai Lama's Visit to the United Kingdom*, The Office of Tibet, May 1993, p 6)

Meanwhile, the continuance of Tibetan Buddhism, uprooted from its historical environment, is sustained by various means. Tibetan refugees have been resettled in India, Nepal and Bhutan with 83 schools established for children across the world. Across the world 117 monasteries have been established. In Dharamsala a Tibetan Medical and Astrological Institute, a library of Tibetan Works and Archives and a Tibetan Institute of Performing Arts have been founded. Such initiatives not only sustain the cultural and religious life of an exiled community, but also offer enrichment to a wider world. This helps, albeit in a small way, to compensate for the deaths of 1.2 million Tibetans, the imprisonment and torture of thousands of religious and political prisoners, the destruction of 6,000 monasteries and the outlawing of the teaching and study of Buddhism in Tibet!

Personal encounters

It was an ironic experience to be offered a children's book on the life of the Buddha, produced by a Buddhist publishing group located at a Tibetan Buddhist Centre in the United Kingdom, in the Tibetan Institute at Sarnath. It was also humbling to be thanked for my interest in the Buddhist religion, when I had taken the time of an important Tibetan official and was, myself, no more than a passing westerner possessing equal amounts of curiosity and cheek. In answer to my question of how the situation of suffering, domination and exile could best be dealt with, he replied: 'By continuing to spread the word of what was happening, pray and hope for the future.' A salutary and gentle response that, in its unexpected character, faced me with my own western conditioning as a matter for reflection.

Tibetan monks in Dharamsala listening to a talk on the situation in Tibet

A world away, in the offices of Wisdom Publications in London, I was introduced to the tulku of Lama Yeshe. He was already known to me, through talking to a nun at one of the western centres that he had established. In her broad Lancashire accent, and while making tea, she described to me the transition, in her later years, from neighbourhood life in a Lancashire town to ordination as a nun in Tibetan robes. In the telling, her respect and affection for the lama who ordained her became apparent.

It comes as something of a shock to a western mind to accommodate the relationship of these two events from a Buddhist perspective, and to become aware of the karmic significance involved. After all, without the Chinese invasion of Tibet, none of these small, anecdotal circumstances would have occurred. Such is the mystery of things, and the influence of large-scale political change on individual lives as it ripples across the globe.

The propagation of the Dharma

On a broader front, western Buddhists in the Tibetan tradition are engaged in producing materials in the form of videos and books for educational and study purposes, in the hope that Mahayana Buddhism may become known to future generations, and be better understood by adults in the modern world. They are also engaged in the question of lineage, since the preservation of the teachings is a matter of the relationship between guru and disciples. Given that Tibetan is not a language generally available to a worldwide audience, much effort is being spent in providing translators of Tibetan origin to disseminate the speeches of Tibetan lamas in English and other languages. At the same time, the teachers themselves are attempting the transition to a new means of communication. The difficulty of the Tibetan situation has raised some debate as to the adaptation of Tibetan Buddhism to western society as well as the influence of modern society on Tibetan Buddhists. As one commentator critically observes:

> Some Tibetan lamas have succeeded in establishing themselves in the Western world, where they have discovered the existence of a potential following among Western 'truth seekers' with predilections for Buddhist or general theosophical ideas. The successful ones seem to be those who have learned to adapt their ideas and teachings to what is expected of them – namely, a minimum of intellectual preparation and the practice of meditation in order to achieve a kind of equipoise in the affairs of this world.
>
> This would seem to be quite desirable so far as it goes, but it is something rather different from the main preoccupation of Tibetan Buddhist practice, which has always offered a transcendent – not a this-worldly – ideal to those who are intellectually and morally prepared, and to those who are not so prepared the prospect of improved this-worldly conditions in a future life, achieved by the accumulation of personal merits. These are the

ideals still kept in mind by the majority of Tibetans in exile, and these are mainly simple folk, whose religion is quite properly one of faith in the Buddhas and supporting divinities and of the practice of meritorious acts. The reciting of invocations to chosen divinities as one tells one's string of 108 beads, the turning of the prayer wheel in supplication to the Lord of Compassion, Avalokiteshvara, and the making of offerings to those who are qualified to recite the scriptures on one's behalf remain the main religious occupations of Tibetan lay folk in the settlements established in India. The few who feel the need for a higher ideal and are free to pursue it must needs go on pilgrimage looking for a suitable teacher, who is certainly still to be found, although the circumstances of life in exile make such a quest far more difficult than it ever was in Tibet itself, and it must be remembered that those who might once have gone on such a quest now tend to go in pursuit of modern forms of education.

(David Snellgrove in Dumoulin and Maraldo, *Buddhism in the Modern World*, Collier Books, New York, 1976, p 291)

Tibetan buddhists outside their tent

—— Theravada Buddhism today ——

Modern influences

The most significant effect on Theravada Buddhism has been the impact of western society and values in the twentieth century. Modern influences have stressed the need for Buddhist teachings to be seen as scientific, and adaptable to worldwide social conditions. In major urban centres its 'religiosity', and adaptation over the course of its history to folklore and local belief, has been played down, in order to make it acceptable to western ways of thinking. The Buddha has been presented as 'the greatest discoverer and scientist of all time', and 'a social reformer bent on liberalising the Brahmanical society of his own day'. The Buddha's teachings have been slanted towards the social purpose of modernising society, and effective social reform, rather than the pursuit of the transcendental goal of enlightenment. Effectively, as in the United Kingdom with Protestant Christianity, Buddhism has tended to shed its cosmological doctrines and meditative emphasis in favour of a more acceptable and pragmatic vision. In effect, this amounts to a form of 'Protestant Buddhism', which presents the Buddha as the exemplar of modern knowledge, as this quote illustrates:

> The Buddha was the first great scientist to appear among men. The Buddha discovered what scientists have only now discovered that there is nothing called matter or mind existing separately in this world but they are the result of forces which continually cause them to come into operation and that they dissolved and came into operation again . . . .
> (Dr. G.P. Malalasekera, quoted in R. Gombrich, *Theravada Buddhism*, Routledge and Keegan Paul, 1988, p 196)

Buddhism and nationalism

In traditionally Theravadin countries like Thailand, Burma, Sri Lanka and Laos, the question of the relationship between religion and national identity has always been important. In a shrinking world which has seen major political and economic changes during the twentieth century, the role of Buddhism has been an important feature of the development of these countries. The monastic Sangha's role, in particular, has been a matter of concern in the face of modernisation, given the possibility of marginalisation.

Efforts have been made to ensure that Buddhism remains a significant intellectual and cultural influence. In Sri Lanka, Thailand and Cambodia, attempts have been made to set up Buddhist Universities. Five have been established since the Second World War; students are encouraged to relate Buddhist doctrines to their contemporary situation, as a training for effective service in society.

There has also been a rebirth of religious vitality amongst lay people. In Thailand in particular, a programme of Dhamma education has increased significantly in modern times. Equally, meditation-orientated Sanghas in Burma and Thailand have sought to revive lay practice. Since the Second World War over 200 meditation centres have been established in Burma. During the 1960s and 70s this revival spread to Thailand and was reinforced by teachers' establishing monasteries, where disciplined meditation practice is seen as reviving the vitality of the monastic Sangha. One example of this is the Forest Retreat Order of Ajahn Chah, which is now established in the West, and has been referred to earlier.

Missionary activity

Buddhist mission has also been a focus of renewal. Initially, its main concern was to restore Buddhist holy places in India; this developed into the re-propagation of Buddhism in India and the publishing of Buddhist literature in English. This mission has now developed, to include seeing the West as an important area of missionary activity. The impetus for this emerged most obviously from the Sixth Great Buddhist Council, where two themes dominated: first, that Christianity and western culture were declining, and Buddhism's 'scientific' approach made it the religion most acceptable to modern society. Second, that Buddhist ethics provided a stabilising influence in a world of continual conflict.

There have been setbacks to all these initiatives, however. Laos and Cambodia have been engulfed by political turmoil. Sri Lanka and Burma have both experienced social and political difficulties which have destabilised national progress. Thailand has to remain wary of the influence of western capitalism on its social fabric and values. Nevertheless, Buddhism still exists as a vital force in the national

identities of these nations, and is becoming recognised in the West as
an alternative source of vision and values.

The Friends of the
Western Buddhist Order

The Friends of the Western Buddhist Order differ from most other
forms of Buddhist organisation in many respects, the most important
being that they are specifically committed to the ideals and practices
of Buddhism in a form that is effective in the conditions of modern
western industrialised society.

It was founded in 1968, by the Ven. Sangharakshita, as a western
Sangha. At the heart of the organisation is the Order itself. This consists of men and women who have gone for refuge to the Three
Jewels, and accepted Sangharakshita as their spiritual teacher. In
this sense, the Western Buddhist Order has established its own tradition, not dependent on, but related to, other branches of Buddhism.

The Three Jewels emblem of the FWBO

Upon ordination, members are invested with a *kesa*, a strip of white brocade worn around the neck, with the emblem of the Three Jewels embroidered on it. If Order members have undertaken to follow a celibate life, the kesa is gold in colour. These are worn at FWBO gatherings, and on occasions when an Order member is representing the FWBO. An Order member also receives a new name, taken from the Sanskrit language, to signify spiritual rebirth and their belonging to the Sangha. It indicates their aspiration to progress in the spiritual life. Thus, for example, 'Bodhananda', meaning the 'Bliss of Enlightenment'.

An FWBO order member teaching at a Buddhist centre

Male Order members are known as Dharmacharis, and female Order members as Dharmacharinis, meaning 'Dharma Farers' or 'those who practise the Dharma'. Order members are not monks or nuns in the traditional sense of being mendicants, but neither are they lay members. The lifestyles of Order members vary, and there are no rules apart from the precepts. Some Order members work full-time for the FWBO, usually teaching and running centres; others work in Right Livelihood businesses, attached to the organisation and seeking to promote its aims. These may be connected with publishing, running bookshops or cafes, and so on. This is a form of outreach, concerned with living an ethical life and supporting the Order itself. Other Order members may work outside the movement, but seek to bring their Buddhist commitment to their professional life, as this comment from a hospital psychiatrist shows:

> If my bleep goes off I use it as a cue to check my breath. I find that useful, like building up little islands of mindfulness into my day.

Sangha and spiritual friendship

The FWBO believes that the Sangha should not be mendicant, because this will hinder the spreading of the Dharma. As one Order member explains:

> For instance, monks aren't allowed to handle money. So, if you're a monk, and you want to travel around the country giving talks on Buddhism, you have to make elaborate arrangements to pay your train fares. The rule is a hindrance. Anagarika Dharmapala (the founder of the Mahabodhi Society) had this problem. Thinking that following the full Vinaya might hamper his work, he did not take the Bhikkhu Ordination. He followed a much simpler form of ethical code, which he thought would allow him to be as effective as possible. After all, what is important is that you are really able to practise Buddhism, and not that a tenpenny piece never crosses you palm.
> (Dharmachari Vessantara in P.Connolly and C. Erricker (eds.), *The Presence and Practice of Buddhism*, W.S.I.H.E., 1985, p 60)

They also feel that it encourages exaggerated deference to a group seen as the religious professionals, diminishes the expectations of the lay person, and is not conducive to a sense of inherent spiritual equality.

The Sangha is therefore understood in a distinctive way, as the following passage explains. It is:

> The totality of those who have 'Gone For Refuge' . . . the spiritual community. It is the absolute contrast to the social group which is a network of need-based relationships. The Sangha comes into being when people experience together their common commitment to the highest of ideals and feel a mutual concern and friendliness. It is only to the extent that there is real metta, true friendliness, that there is Sangha. And it is this spirit of

friendship which is the crucial element in the spiritual life.
(Dharmachari Subhuti, *Buddhism For Today*, Element Books, 1983, p 87)

Mitras

Mitra is the word for 'friend', and denotes Friends of the Order. These are individuals who form an association with the Order without being full Order members. They declare their openness to the movement, and Order members reciprocate by accepting them as mitras. Their involvement may vary from occasional contact through attending classes, to going on retreats or working in one of the FWBO cooperatives, and living in a community. However, it is a positive commitment to practising meditation and learning about the Dharma. Mitras are expected to follow the Buddhist Path and support the development of the movement in an active way. There is a small ceremony for new mitras, at which they make an offering of a flower, a candle and incense before the Buddha image, during a puja.

Positive Buddhism

The FWBO believes that the Buddha's message should be presented in a positive way, such that it is seen as enhancing the society it is in, rather than being separate from it. They emphasise the positive counterpart of each precept. So, for example, the first precept: 'I undertake to refrain form harming living beings', is balanced by, 'With deeds of loving kindness I purify my body'. In concert with this, it welcomes western literature (such as the work of Goethe and William Blake) which represents teachings seen as supporting the Buddhist vision. It accentuates qualities such as good communication, creativity and active involvement in society as ways in which the aim of spiritual evolution can be achieved.

> Whilst we don't ignore the Buddha's teachings on dukkha, we stress that Buddhism is a Path leading to higher and more satisfying mental states. For instance, one traditional formulation of the Dharma which we often talk about is the 'spiral path'. It begins when you see the unsatisfactoriness of ordinary mundane life, which gives you confidence in the Buddha's analysis of the human predicament. With that confidence you practise the precepts and meditation wholeheartedly. This purifies your mind

and leads to higher mental states: joy, rapture, calm and bliss – each state higher than the last – until a total psychic integration is achieved. On the basis of this arises insight into the nature of Reality. This enables you to 'see through' mundane life, so you no longer cling to it. Its waves no longer overwhelm you, or even ruffle your mind. The path culminates in the knowledge that you are completely free from even the subtlest predisposition to future suffering.

(Dharmachari Vessantara, in P. Connolly and C. Erricker (eds)
The Presence and Practice of Buddhism, W.S.I.H.E. 1985, p 67)

The FWBO in India

The FWBO has also been involved in the revival of Buddhism in India among the so-called Untouchables.

The Untouchables are a class of being who are outside caste altogether. A vast congeries of communities and tribes, they are traditionally regarded as being less than human: unfit for education or religious instruction, often even refused the use of the roads. They live in ghettoes just outside the villages and towns, cut off from the rest of the people, expected to perform the most odious tasks, such as scavenging, cleaning lavatories, performing execution, and burning the dead. 'Polluted' from birth, their duty is to perform all the chores that would otherwise bring pollution to the caste Hindu. Above all they must not allow themselves to pollute him through physical, or even visual, contact.

(Nagabodhi, FWBO Newsletter No. 54)

The Buddhist mission to the Untouchables was originally started by Dr. Bhim Ambedkar, himself an Untouchable, who conducted a campaign for social reform as a lawyer and member of the Indian Parliament. He presented the 'Hindu Code Bill' to the Indian Parliament in the late 1940s and early 50s. Its rejection led him to seek an alternative religion for both himself and fellow Untouchables. This brought him into contact with Ven. Sangharakshita, who was also concerned with the role of religion in establishing a just society and spiritual renewal. However, they were both of the opinion that a new Buddhist movement was required to be the vehicle of this vision. At its centre was the concept of the 'Dhamma worker', committed to realising the social ideals of Buddhism, unrestricted by the traditional monastic code.

In October 1956, Ambedkar converted to Buddhism, taking the refuges and precepts from the most senior monk in India, along with 5,000 of his followers. This number increased to about four million in the following months. Dr. Ambedkar, however, was a sick man, and died just five weeks after his conversion leaving the movement without a leader. Sangharakshita committed himself to holding the movement together, despite vituperative opposition from sections of the Indian press.

After 1977 the FWBO, already established in the West, was a prime motivating force sustaining the missionary activity begun by Ambedkar in India. The movement is known as 'Trailokya Bauhdda Mahasangha Sahayak Gana', and its main centres are in Pune and Ahmedabad. Its teachings emphasise spiritual practice and the relevance of Buddhism in the modern world. In contrast to other forms of traditional Buddhism, it is particularly socio-politically oriented, with a strong emphasis on ethical teachings, social identity and the need for vernacular preaching and teaching. Its character is well illustrated by the following passage:

> The local group usually meets weekly or monthly to recite simple texts ... sometimes in Pali, more often in Marathi or Hindi, and to listen to explanations of Buddhism. In villages the converts still live in their special area outside the village proper; the temple or shrine of their deity, usually the goddess Mariai or Mariamma, goddess of smallpox and cholera, has in most cases been changed into a Buddhist mandir, small statues and pictures of Buddha and Ambedkar replacing the shapeless stone of the goddess. In cities the majority cluster in slums, where a small hut is set aside for the same purpose.
>
> (H. Dumoulin and J. Maraldo (eds), *Buddhism in the Modern World*, Collier, 1976, p 143)

The writer goes on to remark, however, that such converts often retain a hatred of Hinduism as the cause and symbol of their former degradation, despite the Buddhist doctrines of universal love and compassion.

In conclusion, we may say that the twentieth century has been a time of upheaval and progressive change for Buddhism, as its traditional centres have been subjected to different political and economic influences. Its missionary activity has increased, but it is too early to say whether it will ultimately have any significant effect. Its contacts with communism, capitalism and advances in scientific knowledge have placed it in a position similar to that of other world faiths in a world of rapid change. The relevance of the Buddha's teaching, however, does not seem to have diminished.

FURTHER READING

The Dhammapada Narada Thera, John Murray, 1972. This is one of a number of translations of this popular and important collection of some of the Buddha's sayings.

What the Buddha Taught W. Rahula, Wisdom Books, 1985. The latest reprint of an authoritative and readable introduction to the Buddha's fundamental teachings.

The Buddha M. Carrithers, Oxford University Press, 1983. A valuable account of the life of the Buddha and the development of his teaching.

The Buddhist Handbook J. Snelling, Rider, 1987. An introduction to the main schools of Buddhism, their teachings and practices.

An Introduction to Buddhism: teachings, history and practices P. Harvey, Cambridge University Press, 1990. A more detailed introduction to the tradition as a whole.

Theravada Buddhism: a social history from ancient Benares to modern Colombo R. Gombrich, Routledge, 1988. A more detailed investigation of the development of this branch of Buddhism.

Mahayana Buddhism: the doctrinal foundations P. Williams, Routledge, 1989. A survey of the diversity and complexity of the Mahayana.

Being Nobody, Going Nowhere Ayya Khema, Wisdom Publications,

1987. A very useful and practical guide to Buddhist meditation by a Buddhist nun.

A Guide to the Buddhist Path Ven. Sangharakshita, Windhorse Publications, 1990. A collection of talks given by the author on aspects of Buddhist teaching and practice, from the perspective of the FWBO.

Zen Mind, Beginner's Mind Shunryu Suzuki, Weatherhill, 1982. A collection of influential talks on Zen meditation and practice by a respected Japanese master.

The Buddhist Directory The Buddhist Society, London. This directory is updated every few years. It gives information of Buddhist groups and centres in the UK and Ireland.

The World of Buddhism H. Bechert and R. Gombrich (eds), Thames and Hudson, 1984. A large-format, beautifully illustrated survey of Buddhism.

Buddhists in Britain Today D. Cush, Hodder and Stoughton, 1990. A very readable collection of interviews with British Buddhists.

Buddhism (A Student's Approach to World Religions series) D. Cush, Hodder and Stoughton, 1994. A substantial but readable introduction to Buddhism.

Buddhism P. Morgan, Batsford, 1987. A dictionary with explanations of key terms in Buddhism.

USEFUL ADDRESSES

The Buddhist Society, 58 Ecclestone Square, London, SW1V 1PH.

Amaravati Buddhist Monastery, Great Gaddesden, Hemel Hempstead, Hertfordshire, HP1 3BZ.

Throssel Hole Priory, Carrshield, Hexham, Northumberland, NE47 8AL.

The Friends of the Western Buddhist Order, Lesingham House, Surlingham, Norwich, NR14 7AL.

Kagyu Samye Ling Tibetan Centre, Eskdalemuir, Langholm, Dumfriesshire, Scotland, DG13 0QL.

GLOSSARY

Note: (P) and (S) refer to Pali and Sanskrit respectively.

Abhidamma (P), **Abhidharma** (S): Buddhist philosophical texts
Amitabha: Buddha of the Pure Land
Anagarika: literally 'wandering one', a truth-seeker
Anapanasati: meditation of the breath
Anatta: the doctrine of no-self
Anicca: change, impermanence
Anuradhapura: ancient capital of Sri Lanka, and a place of pilgrimage
Ashoka: Buddhist Emperor of India
Avalokiteshvara (Chenrezig): Bodhisattva of Compassion
Arahant (Arhat): one who has achieved liberation

Bardo: the state between death and rebirth mentioned in the *Bardo Thodol* (*Tibetan Book of the Dead*)
Bhavana: mental development or meditation
Bhikkhu (M), **Bhikkhuni** (F): A monk or nun in the Theravadin tradition
Bodhi: Enlightenment
Bodh-Gaya: the place of the Buddha's Enlightenment
Bodhidharma: an Indian monk who took Buddhism to China in the 6th century CE
Bodhisattva: a being with the essence of enlightenment
Buddha: Enlightened One

Chela: pupil of a guru

Dalai Lama: head of Tibetan Buddhism; incarnation of the Bodhisattva Avalokiteshvara

Dana: literally, 'giving' or 'generosity'; the only meal of the day for Theravadin monks

Dependent Origination: the process of the cycle of samsaric existence, also called 'conditioned co-production'

Devas: gods

Dhamma (P), **Dharma** (S): the teaching of the Buddha; the Truth or Law

Dhammapada: popular collection of the Buddha's teachings

Dharmachari: literally, 'Dharma-farer'; the title given to Order members of the FWBO

Dharamsala: the Indian Himalayan town where the Dalai Lama has his palace in exile

Dukkha: suffering, unsatisfactoriness, dis-ease; the First Noble Truth

Darsana: a teaching or 'sermon'; discourse of the Buddha

Guru: spiritual teacher or master

Hui-neng: Sixth Patriarch of the Zen tradition

Jatakas: tales of the Buddha's former lives

Kamma (P), **Karma** (S): literally means 'action'; The Law of Cause and Effect

Kangyur: Tibetan Scriptures

Karuna: compassion

Kathina: literally means 'difficult' or 'frame'. The robe-giving ceremony in Theravada Buddhism

Koan: a 'riddle' or technique used in Zen Buddhism

Kusala (P), **Kausalya** (S): skilfulness

Lao Tzu: Taoist teacher

Losar: Tibetan New Year

Lotus Sutra, or **'Saddharmapundarika'**: literally the 'Lotus of the True Law'; important Mahayana Scripture

Lumbini: the place of the Buddha's birth

Magga: literally 'path'; refers to the Eightfold Path in Buddhism; the fourth Noble Truth

Mahayana: literally 'The Great Way'; one of the main branches of Buddhism

Manjushri: Bodhisattva of Wisdom
Mandala: literally means 'circle'; a design used for meditation in Mahayana Buddhism
Mara: Lord of Death
Maya: illusion or creative play of the universe
Mendicant: one who relies on others for his material and physical needs
Merit: reward for good deed; store of goodness
Metta: loving kindness.
Milinda: king who features in the Theravada Scriptures in dialogue with the Buddhist monk, Nagasena
Mitra: literally 'friend'; term used by the FWBO
Mondo: story used in Zen Buddhism

Nagasena: Buddhist monk
Nibbana (P), **Nirvana** (S): literally 'to extinguish'; enlightenment
Nirodha: the third Noble Truth; letting go of suffering

Padmasambhava: Tibetan saint
Pali: language of the Theravada Scriptures, also used by the Buddha
Paranibbana (P), **Paranirvana**: passing into Nirvana upon death
Prajna: Wisdom
Precepts: Rules of behaviour
Pretas: Hungry ghosts
Puja: worship

Relics: holy objects; remains of the Buddha or a great Buddhist teacher
Refuge: refers to the Three Jewels as Refuges; that in which one can trust

Sadhu: holy man
Sakyamuni: title given to the Buddha, literally 'Sage of the Sakya clan'
Samanera: literally 'child of a Samana' (religious seeker); refers to a novice monk
Samatha: calm, inner peace; form of meditation technique
Samsara: cycle of existence
Samudaya: the second Noble Truth; the origin of suffering
Sangha: the Buddhist Community or Order
Shastras: commentaries on the Buddha's teachings

Siddhatta Gotama (P), **Siddhartha Gautama** (S): name of the historical Buddha

Sila: Ethical Conduct; second part of the Eightfold Path

Sima: ordination area in Theravada Buddhism

Skandhas: the five elements that constitute a person

Stupa: Burial mound or building to house relics; also called a chorten or chedi

Sukha: happiness, bliss or ease; the opposite of dukkha

Sukhavati: the Pure Land

Sunyata: Voidness

Sutta (P), **Sutra** (S): literally means 'thread'; name for the Buddhist Scriptures

Tanha: thirst or craving

Tantra: form of Tibetan Buddhist practice and name of a type of scripture

Tao: literally 'The Way'; a Chinese tradition that influenced Zen Buddhism

Tara: female Bodhisattva, 'Mother of Compassion'; there are two Taras, Green Tara and White Tara

Tathagatha: literally 'Thus Gone One'; title given to the Buddha

Tengyur: name of the Shastras in Tibetan Buddhism

Theravada: 'Way of the Elders'; branch of Buddhism

Tsongkhapa: Tibetan saint and teacher

Tulku: the rebirth of a great teacher in Tibetan Buddhism, especially the Dalai Lama

Upaya: skill in means

Uposatta: weekly days of observance based on the lunar cycle; full-moon days are the most important

Vihara: Monastic residence

Vinaya: code of Monastic Discipline laid down by the Buddha

Vipassana: insight, form of meditation

Wesak: Theravada festival celebrating birth, enlightenment and death of the Buddha

Zen: Japanese form of Buddhism; from the Chinese 'Ch'an' and Sanskrit 'Dhyana', meaning meditation.

INDEX

Abbreviations:
P – Pali; S – Sanskrit;
m – male; f – female